ROSIE
and
MRS. AMERICA

PERCEPTIONS OF WOMEN
IN THE 1930S AND 1940S

Catherine Gourley

Twenty-First Century Books • Minneapolis

For Jo and Ted Gourley, whose stories of their
childhood and youth always fired my imagination

Twenty-First Century Books
A division of Lerner Publishing Group, Inc.
241 First Avenue North
Minneapolis, MN 55401 U.S.A.

Website address: www.lernerbooks.com

Library of Congress Cataloging-in-Publication Data

Gourley, Catherine, 1950–
    Rosie and Mrs. America : perceptions of women in the 1930s and 1940s / by Catherine Gourley.
        p.   cm. — (Images and issues of women in the Twentieth Century)
    Includes bibliographical references and index.
    ISBN: 978–0–8225–6804–9 (lib. bdg. : alk. paper)
    1. Women—United States—History—20th century. 2. Women—United States—Social conditions—20th century.
3. Women—United States—Social life and customs—20th century. 4. Popular culture—United States—History—20th century.
5. Nineteen thirties. 6. Nineteen forties. I. Title.
HQ1420.G68 2008
305.40973'09043—dc22   2006028984

Manufactured in the United States of America
1 2 3 4 5 6 – JR – 13 12 11 10 09 08

Contents

It is Labor Day, 1943—but there is no day off for these patriotic steelworkers who enthusiastically report to work knowing that their labors are supporting the effort of the United States in World War II (1939–1945). The press affectionately dubbed such working women Rosies— short for Rosie the Riveter.

AUTHOR'S NOTE

In Frank Capra's 1939 film *Mr. Smith Goes to Washington (below)*, the female lead character is a secretary called Saunders. She is one of the boys—so much so that no one knows her first name. Saunders teaches the junior senator everything he needs to know about the workings of Congress and how a bill becomes law. She teaches him too how to beat a corrupt political opponent. Without Saunders, Mr. Smith would have fled back to his home state in disgrace.

In 1939 images of women in the popular media, especially film and magazine fiction, often emphasized a wisecracking career woman. Indeed, during the first three decades of the twentieth century, women's place in the workforce increased to about 25 percent. Advertisements, on the other hand, usually portrayed American women as nurturing housewives and mothers. And in many ways, this too was a reality. The 1941 bombing of Pearl Harbor, Hawaii, however, triggered a dramatic shift in American lives from an uneasy peace to war. In one of his 1942 fireside chats, President Roosevelt said, "In some communities, employers dislike to employ women. . . . We can no longer afford to indulge such prejudices or practices."

To convince U.S. industry and women, too, to do their patriotic duty to help the United States win World War II (1939–1945), the government created a new media image: Rosie the Riveter. Rosie was a tireless and patriotic woman, but she wasn't just a riveter who built airplanes and warships. She typed letters in government offices, engineered trains, flew airplanes, and planted Victory Gardens.

This book is the third in a series on women's images and issues. It focuses on the decades of the 1930s and 1940s. To research the book, I traveled back in time to search for the real-life Rosies and Saunders. Specifically, I hunted for answers to two questions: How did the popular media of the past portray women? Were those images of women accurate or misleading?

An image can be visual, such as a photograph, a painting, or a film. But images are also print documents, including letters, newspaper articles, short stories, and novels. In searching for women's images as well as the issues important to women during the 1930s and 1940s, I read the yellowed pages of magazines. I listened to the static-laced voices of radio broadcasts. I watched Hollywood films. I studied advertisements and the posters and photographs created by the U.S. Office of War Information. My research was part of the journey, and I loved it. But I also discovered something about myself.

I had much in common with these women whose histories I touched. I never attended one of First Lady Eleanor Roosevelt's press conferences for women. I did not photograph migrant women picking peas in a California field. Nor did I swing a baseball bat as a member of the All-American Girls Professional Baseball League or play clarinet with one of the all-girl swing bands so popular during the war years. Even so, the dreams and disappointments of women in the 1930s and 1940s were often the same dreams and disappointments I had and have still.

Throughout the twentieth century, media images—whether fact or fiction, stereotypical or sensationalized—influenced women's perception of themselves. But the reaction was not always blind acceptance. Many women rebelled against the images society had painted for them. Their rebellion not only made headlines but also opened doors for other women to express their own individuality.

The conflicting images of popular culture and the ways women reacted to those images is what this series is all about. As you read, you too will travel back in time. I hope you'll return to the present with greater understanding of how popular culture may have influenced your mother, your grandmother, perhaps even your great-grandmother. More important, I hope you'll see yourself reflected within these pages and understand that you—not society—hold the paintbrush that creates the person you become.

—*Catherine Gourley*

We are going through a great crisis in this country. . . . The women have a big part to play if we are coming through successfully.

—First Lady Eleanor Roosevelt, 1937,
pictured above with her husband, President Franklin D. Roosevelt

On the morning of March 4, 1933,

Eleanor Roosevelt woke early, feeling "deeply troubled." In a few hours, her husband would take the oath of office for president of the United States. For the past three years, many Americans had suffered terribly through an economic depression. Millions were hungry and homeless. Eleanor Roosevelt had confidence that Franklin Delano Roosevelt (FDR) could lead Americans to a better life. Although she was hopeful for the country, she was unhappy for herself. Her husband's election, she believed, would put an end to any personal life of her own.

On inauguration morning, she planned to take her dogs for a brisk walk before breakfast. And so, accompanied by her Scottish terrier and her German shepherd, Roosevelt rode the elevator to the lobby of the Mayflower Hotel. Secret Service agents tried to talk her out of walking alone at dawn through the still-empty streets of Washington, D.C., but she refused their protection. While her husband had been governor of New York, she had refused the protection of the state police as well. She did not fear the American people, she argued. She had always walked among them. Besides, she enjoyed exercise. On this morning, in her last hours of freedom (for she had begun to think of the White House as a prison), she intended to walk her dogs by herself.

FDR's campaign song had been "Happy Days Are Here Again," but the happy days had not yet arrived. The winter of 1932–1933 had been bitter for the hungry and the homeless. Nor were the skies above clear, as the song's lyrics stated. Instead, gray clouds threatened rain. Eleanor's mood that morning was just as gloomy. She had lived in Washington previously when Franklin had served as secretary of the navy. Also, as the niece of former president Theodore Roosevelt, she had watched her aunt perform the duties of First Lady. Now Eleanor was to assume the same role. She knew what society expected of her: to be a gracious hostess, well dressed and well behaved, supporting her husband in all of his political policies. Her ideas and viewpoints must be secondary to his, if expressed at all. She understood, too, that the eyes of women across America would be watching and judging her performance. Eleanor Roosevelt didn't lack social graces. She knew how to pour tea and how to manage a house. That wasn't what troubled her. Rather, she hated having to give up her freedom, including the right to express her own opinions.

FDR called Eleanor his "Missus," but she was not a typical American housewife. She was independent, earning her own money as a teacher and a writer. In matters that concerned her most—the welfare of children and families and the rights of women and minority races—she spoke her mind. She drove her own car and often lived apart from her husband. During FDR's campaign, the press often criticized her behavior and ideas as unwifely.

On election night, when Eleanor Roosevelt had congratulated her husband on his victory, he said to her, "I wish I knew what you were really thinking and feeling." She never told him. However, to her intimate friend, reporter Lorena Hickok, she confessed that she wished Franklin had never run for the office. "I never wanted to be a president's wife," she said.

After winning the election, FDR had asked his Missus to give up her teaching position at Todhunter, the New York City private school for girls of which she was part owner. Although she hated doing it, she agreed. He asked her to give up her membership in social and political organizations, such as the

First Lady Eleanor Roosevelt is shown seated beneath a sign that expressed the theme of the 1933 Chicago World's Fair: A Century of Progress. The fair emphasized not only the nation's achievements but also its bright future—an important reassurance to a country in the throes of the Great Depression (1929–1942).

League of Women Voters. Again, she agreed. Her loss of freedom had already begun.

Perhaps as she walked her dogs that inauguration morning through the nation's capital, Eleanor came to terms with her new life. Like it or not, Franklin had been elected. And the press would likely continue to criticize her, no matter what she said or did. With Meggie and Major at her heels, she returned to the Mayflower Hotel, determined to make the best of things. She breakfasted, then dressed in an elegant velvet gown and coat she had purchased for the occasion of becoming America's new First Lady.

during the first two decades of the twentieth century, women in the United States had achieved a good deal of independence. They had won the right to vote. The number of young women graduating from colleges soared, and as a result, more women had entered professions that previously had been considered "for men only." These included law, medicine, journalism, and government. Women's fashions had changed dramatically, as well. Gone were tight-fitting, rib-constricting corsets. Gone were long, sweeping skirts and, with them, high-buttoned shoes and dark cotton stockings. Gone, too, were many social restrictions on what a good girl might or might not do in public. During the 1920s, women drove cars, smoked cigarettes, danced the Charleston, and kissed the young men who courted them. They flew airplanes. Elinor Smith was just seventeen years old when she flew her biplane over New York's Long Island for 13 hours, 16 minutes, and 45 seconds to set a new endurance record for flying solo.

Elinor Smith set many aviation records. At the age of fifteen, she was the youngest woman to fly solo. At sixteen she became the youngest American to earn a pilot's license. At nineteen she was chosen over Amelia Earhart as Best Woman Pilot of 1930. That same year, both Bellanca and Fairchild companies hired her as their first woman test pilot.

All across the United States, the Great Depression left people jobless and without enough to eat (above: men waiting in line for free food—New York City, 1932) and eventually without a permanent place to live (below: a Hooverville settlement for temporary lodging at the edge of a town dump—Bakersfield, California, 1936).

The adventurous days of that decade, however, had ended when the stock market crashed in October 1929. Overnight it seemed, though in truth the trouble had been brewing for years, America's banks and businesses lost most of their financial investments. Families lost their savings. This was more than just an economic slump. It was the beginning of what would come to be known as the Great Depression. Months then years passed, and still more banks closed, more factories shut down, and more people lost their jobs and their homes. By inauguration day, 1933, the United States was a nation in turmoil. One out of every four people was out of work. In cities the homeless flocked to empty lots and railroad yards where they built shacks of cardboard and scrap pieces of wood and tin. They called these shantytowns Hoovervilles, after President Herbert Hoover, who had been in office for the past four years but who had not been able to get the country out of its predicament. At night they covered themselves with newspapers, which they scornfully called Hoover blankets.

by inauguration day, 1933, the United States was a nation in turmoil. One out of every four people was out of work.

The price of most everything had dropped. In New York City, for example, a loaf of bread dropped from approximately eight cents to a nickel. A quart of milk that had cost fourteen cents was now a dime. For six dollars a mother could buy a wool sweater and a pair of shoes for her child. But even these low prices were often beyond what many families could afford. To put the prices in perspective, a typical factory worker or office secretary earned under twenty dollars a week. A schoolteacher or an insurance salesman might earn a couple of dollars more. Most families on a budget had to carefully choose how to spend their money. A visit to the dentist to have a sore tooth drilled might cost one dollar, but that same dollar could purchase a blanket to cover a bed in which two, three, or more might sleep.

Of course, not everyone was out of work and poor. New automobiles still rolled off the assembly lines. Hollywood movies still attracted audiences. Newsstands displayed many dozens of magazines, including detective fiction and a popular new type of reading material, comic books. The price of a radio had dropped by almost 50 percent since the 1920s, and thousands of families somehow found enough nickels and dimes to purchase one.

The "inner turmoil" that Eleanor Roosevelt experienced on inauguration day was something that many women in the United States were also experiencing as a result of the Great Depression. The media sent women a clear message: because jobs are scarce, you belong in the home, not in the workplace. A woman who worked was viewed as stealing a job from a man. Many, like Mrs. Roosevelt, were reluctant to give up their careers and their independence. The choice, however, often wasn't theirs to make. Employers let their women workers go or reduced their wages. When a job opening occurred, employers tended to hire men rather than women. A single woman who worked was generally more acceptable than a married woman who worked. In some professions, such as teaching, when a woman married, it was understood she would give up her job. Some people even blamed women's entry into the job market in the 1920s as one of the causes of the Depression in the 1930s.

A 1930s advertisement for Ladies' Home Journal suggests that a new term be added to the English language: homemaker. It goes on to present a lengthy list of qualities that such a woman must possess.

The economic depression impacted other choices women made about their lives as well. For example, some postponed marriage and stayed home to help their families make ends meet. Married couples often put off having children because they simply didn't have enough money to raise a

Above all and especially during hard times, a woman had to look her best or so the popular media of the times suggested. "The world is very tired of shabby, gloomy-looking people," wrote Samuel Crowther in *Ladies' Home Journal*. "The woman who consciously looks less than her best is going against an

*t*he media sent women a clear message:
you belong in the home, not in the workplace.

family. Others moved into the same apartment or house with their parents or other close relatives as a way to pool limited resources.

Movies, radio programs, magazines, books, comic strips, and even government posters advised a woman how to dress, please her husband, raise her children, and cook her food. Sometimes the advice was how to get a job, but usually the job was in domestic service as a hotel maid, a dressmaker, a cook, or a waitress. "It's Up to the Women" was the title of an article in a 1932 issue of *Ladies' Home Journal* on how women could help restore the country's prosperity. More often than not, her contribution was finding creative ways to turn tasteless leftovers into an appetizing meal.

age-old tradition. And her intentional shabbiness will soon bore her husband, her children, and her friends."

Many American women accepted these ideas as truth. Many others, such as Eleanor Roosevelt, challenged the media. They dared to be different.

Rosie and Mrs. America is part of a series of books on the images and issues that influenced American women during the twentieth century. It focuses on the decades of the 1930s and 1940s. It is a journey back in time to examine how popular culture during the Great Depression and later during World War II influenced the lives of women. It is the story too of how women swept away the stereotypes and changed the way the world perceived them.

Chapter One
Ain't We Got Fun?
Amusements and Diversions in Hard Times

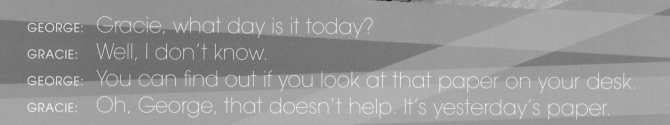

GEORGE: Gracie, what day is it today?

GRACIE: Well, I don't know.

GEORGE: You can find out if you look at that paper on your desk.

GRACIE: Oh, George, that doesn't help. It's yesterday's paper.

—from the 1937 movie *A Damsel in Distress*,
starring comic performers Gracie Allen *(right)* and George Burns *(left)*

In the office of J. Bolling Bumstead,

a serious meeting was taking place. The wealthy railroad owner sat behind his desk and puffed on his cigar. A pretty, petite young woman sat with her back to him. In another chair was a broad-shouldered young man, handsome in his well-tailored suit. "I want you to marry this man!" J. Bolling Bumstead ordered the woman.

"No, Mr. B," the pretty girl answered firmly.

"How dare you refuse a command of mine! When I want a bridge, I build it. When I want a college, I buy it. . . . Don't dare refuse me!"

The young woman whirled around and snapped, "Oh, go climb a stick and holler 'Fire!'" Shocked by her boldness as well as her language, Bumstead and the handsome gent fell off their chairs!

The pretty girl was Blondie Boopadoop. She was a cartoon creation of artist Chic Young. Blondie entered the world of American newspaper comics in 1930. She was a flapper, a carefree youth who spent her nights in dance halls. The readers of the comic strip also suspected she was a gold digger. A gold digger is a woman who believes that money, not love, solves all problems. Among Blondie's many suitors was playboy Dagwood Bumstead. Dagwood was clumsy, and he lacked the business smarts of his railroad tycoon father, J. Bolling. But Blondie didn't care, because one day, Dagwood was sure to inherit his father's wealth.

The comic strip was a flop. The Depression had put so many people out of work that the antics of a money-hungry blonde chasing a bumbling playboy just weren't funny. To save the comic strip, Chic Young changed the story's plotline. Blondie and Dagwood fell in love. Dagwood's furious father and mother refused to allow their son to marry a woman of Blondie's low social class. The courtship and conflict continued week after week in the newspapers across the country. At one

Dagwood and Blondie *comic strip, 1932*

point, Dagwood went on a hunger strike (it was Blondie's idea) to convince his father to change his mind. The hunger strike worked—not in changing J. Bolling's mind but in hooking newspaper readers. Suddenly, people by the thousands began writing letters to their local newspapers, supporting the cartoon marriage. It was as if Blondie and Dagwood were real-life people and not pen and ink drawings.

J. Bolling Bumstead tried everything to chase Blondie away. As a last resort, he presented Dagwood with an ultimatum: if Dagwood married Blondie, J. Bolling would disinherit him. "We'll live on love," Blondie consoled Dagwood.

And so, on the funny pages of February 17, 1933, Dagwood and Blondie got married. The penniless but happy couple soon became the parents of a son, Baby Dumpling. Each week, the family tried hard to make ends meet, which is exactly what most Americans in the 1930s were also trying to do. The comic strip became so popular that when Blondie gave birth to a daughter a few years later, more than 400,000 readers suggested names for the new baby to their local newspapers. *Time* magazine reported: "If Blondie fries an egg in a new-type pan, letters flood in from readers who want to know where she got it."

Blondie had made the transition from the 1920s to the 1930s, from gold digger to Mrs. America, a modern housewife and mother. People loved her for it. Like Blondie, they, too, had changed. Most of them didn't have much money either, and they longed to believe what Blondie had told Dagwood—that love, not money, solved all problems.

"If Blondie fries an egg in a new-type pan, letters flood in from readers who want to know where she got it."

—*Time* magazine, 1949

There was something for everyone in 1930s radio. Uncle Remus read stories for the children. The Lone Ranger, Buck Rogers, or Superman offered adventure, and Amos and Andy or Jack Benny tickled the funny bone. And the daytime soap operas held special appeal for the women.

Welcome to Radioland

Despite the hard years of the Great Depression, people found ways to enjoy life. Families didn't have much money to spend on entertainment, so they stayed home. They found new ways to have fun. They worked on jigsaw puzzles or played parlor games, such as Monopoly. Monopoly players bought and sold property with paper money. Players who couldn't pay their rent lost the deed to their land. Perhaps one reason Monopoly became so popular so quickly in the 1930s was that a person could feel wealthy with a few lucky throws of the dice.

Games such as Monopoly and comic strips such as *Blondie* were distractions from hard times. So, too, was radio. Without spending a lot of money, families could tune in to a concert or a baseball or football game. They could dance in their living rooms and kitchens to the music of a swing band.

Dozens of comedy programs, including the silly antics of Baby Snooks and Little Orphan Annie, brought laughter into the lives of radio listeners. For a little while at least, mothers and fathers forgot to worry about paying the bills.

Radio airwaves had the amazing ability to transport people to distant places. A woman sitting in her farm kitchen in Kansas could imagine herself dancing in a ballroom in Chicago, Illinois. Radioland brought her in contact with people and ideas beyond her small town. She might never have had the opportunity to meet President Roosevelt in person, but by tuning in to his weekly fireside chats, she could hear his voice. It was as if he were right there sitting in the room beside her. Likewise, she might listen in on an interview with a Hollywood movie star or a famous woman from high society. Radio brought these celebrities from faraway places into her home.

Beginning in the 1930s, women's radio programs filled the daytime hours between 9:00 A.M. and 6:00 P.M. These talk shows and interviews introduced a woman to issues and points of view to which she might never have been exposed in her own community, including health, fashions, or even a discussion of wages for working women. More often than not, however, women's programs focused on homemaking and child care. During the Depression years of the 1930s, the message was often "it's up to the women" to make ends meet. During the years of World War II in the 1940s, the message was still "it's up to the women." But the cause was new: to help win the war on the home front by recycling household materials such as tin cans or grease, planting Victory Gardens, or working in a factory.

Radio both entertained and informed. But radio meant something much more for women: it was a new communication technology that opened doors of employment. Many women got their first jobs in radio in the 1920s as program directors. Radio was still a novelty, and many of the small-town stations broadcast for just a few hours a day. The program director planned the day's local programs. She was responsible for finding "talent," people who might speak with knowledge about a particular subject or who could sing or play an instrument. Women who had experience as leaders of community and social service clubs made very good radio program directors. In addition, women usually ran the music schools in their hometowns or sang in their church choirs. As a result, they were acquainted with speakers and performers they could book for an appearance on the radio airwaves.

Some women worked as broadcast engineers at the radio stations, maintaining and repairing the microphones, amplifiers, and transmitting equipment. This usually required a knowledge of mathematics and science. In school, girls ordinarily did not study these subjects, but young men did, and so there were more male than female radio broadcast engineers. Still, those women who had an interest in radio technology learned quickly and often found work with a small-town station. Women also found jobs as radio announcers. They might read the weather, interview a guest, or introduce a performer. Edythe Meserand got her start on the radio airwaves in the 1920s as the "Musical Clock Girl." *The Musical Clock* program aired each morning from six until nine. Periodically throughout the morning, she came on the air to announce the time of day.

The female workers at New York City's WNYC all have an opportunity to be at the microphone at a 1948 gathering to celebrate the radio station's twenty-fifth anniversary.

Local radio stations usually operated on a small budget. Many hired women simply because they could pay a woman less money than a man. By the 1930s, however, radio had grown tremendously. Hundreds of radio stations broadcast for eight hours a day or more. As radio audiences grew, so did the number of radio sponsors, or advertisers. New programs and new stars, more money and, most important of all, millions of new listeners made radio a big business.

Doors that once allowed women to enter the profession began to close as radio gained a higher profile. Prejudices about women surfaced: one, women weren't organized or business minded enough to manage a large staff or keep track of a budget; two, women were opinionated and emotional and, therefore, difficult to work with. These prejudices led to changes in hiring practices at the stations.

Many women who were program directors lost their jobs and became station hostesses instead. A hostess's responsibilities were significantly less important than a program manager's. She answered fan mail or assisted performers as they arrived to do a broadcast, and in general put on a pretty face for the public. Many female announcers discovered that they, too, were out of a job. Polls revealed that listeners preferred men's voices to women's. One reason might have been the broadcasting equipment. In its early years, the microphone tended to distort a person's voice. Women's higher-pitched voices often came across the airwaves as shrill.

The sound of a woman's voice, however, was not the only reason station owners booted them off the airwaves. Advertisers who sponsored radio programs believed—often as a result of a survey they had conducted— that a man's voice suggested authority. Radio listeners could believe what a man said.

The Kate Smith Show, *which began in 1931, soon propelled the outspoken singer to the position of top radio performer in the United States.*

Women, on the other hand, simply weren't decisive or credible.

Edythe Meserand, however, was one of the lucky women of radio. "I had a good radio voice," she said. "It was deep. I enunciated properly and I didn't do it on purpose. I just spoke that way." She wasn't particularly happy sitting in front of a microphone, however. She had no ambition to become a radio personality or star. She was much more

> "I had a good radio voice. It was deep. I enunciated properly and I didn't do it on purpose. I just spoke that way."
>
> —Edythe Meserand, 1990

interested in working behind the scenes, in the executive offices, if possible, producing programs. One of her station managers told her frankly, "You will never be an executive in this organization . . . that's the way it is here."

"He didn't believe in women," Meserand said. But she believed in herself. No one was going to break her spirit. In the years to come, she would help to establish the first-ever radio newsroom for station WOR in New York City. Her job was just as she wanted it—not in front of the mike reporting the news but behind the scenes creating news programs. Her career in radio would last for decades.

Women could become successful as radio personalities if paired with a man. The husband-wife team of George Burns and Gracie Allen became radio favorites. George was serious, the straight man in the comedy act. Gracie was naive. She often misunderstood simple things, such as thinking a Man Wanted poster in a post office was an advertisement for community volunteers.

Only one female comedian made it on her own into the top ten radio comedy shows of the 1930s. Fanny Brice, a former comic stage actress in her forties, played Baby Snooks. Snooks was a little girl whose curiosity in each episode landed her—and her daddy—into mischief. Part of the fun in every episode was anticipating the moment when Daddy's patience would explode.

Hour of Charm

Radio both reinforced stereotypes about women and swept away those stereotypes. The *Hour of Charm* challenged the common thinking that women were too competitive to work together, even to create music. The program featured the first-ever all-girl radio orchestra. Each member was a serious musician who could read music fluently. Talent was not the only qualification to become a member of the orchestra. The man who created the orchestra in 1934 as a radio gimmick was Phil Spitalny. He auditioned women not only for their musical ability but also for their "sweetness and charm." The requirements included that they be unmarried and weigh no more than 122 pounds (55 kilograms). Spitalny also determined how the musicians would dress—in a type of uniform rather than evening gowns—and how they wore their hair. He even controlled their social lives when not performing in the orchestra. *Radioland*, a fan magazine, reported that the orchestra had a committee of five girls who settled all "backstage disputes." This included dating. The article stated: "Whenever a girl wants to go out, she goes to the committee and says, 'I want a date with Mr. So-and-So.' They ask her who the man is, what he does, and for references. If he passes muster, she gets her date. But if the committee feels that it would hurt the orchestra for a member to be seen with that man, the engagement doesn't materialize."

Phil Spitalny and his all-girl orchestra, pictured here in 1938

Radio comedian Fanny Brice dressed as her young girl character, Baby Snooks, pulls British actor Hanley Stafford's tie in a promotional portrait for Brice's radio program, The Baby Snooks Show.

These two female popular radio stars, Gracie Allen and Fanny Brice, played different characters, and yet they shared something in common. Gracie's character was childlike in her logic. Fanny's character was a baby brat. The acts were funny, to be sure. But they also helped perpetrate the misconception that women, like children, needed the protection of a husband or father.

Childlike innocence, however, was not the only female image broadcast over the airwaves. Soap opera heroines contributed another view of women's lives to the public.

Bad News and Misunderstandings

Portia has a problem. Actually, she has lots of problems. Just when she gets one solved, another pops up. However, in the very first episode (1940) of the radio soap opera drama *Portia Faces Life*, the crisis is a doozy. Her handsome husband, Richard Blake, dies under mysterious circumstances. The grieving Portia must raise their son, Dickie, alone. Luckily for her, she's a successful attorney (unlike most real women in the United States in the 1930s and 1940s). She is also a stereotype, says Mona Kent, the woman writer who created her. Portia is a saintly sufferer. She is honest and kind and trusts people she ought not to, such as Arline Harrison, the daughter of the publisher of the *Parkerstown Herald*. When Portia falls in love with her dead husband's best friend, Walter Manning, Arline steals him from her. Nasty!

Portia Faces Life was a popular radio soap opera that aired every day for eleven years (1940–1951). Soap operas got their names from their advertising sponsors, usually the manufacturers of soap detergents. (Portia's sponsor, however, was General Mills, the makers of Raisin Bran cereal.)

Introduced by a male radio announcer, the soap opera aired during the daytime, when the radio audience was mainly women. Most soap opera heroines presented unrealistic images of women. Characters were either pure of heart, like Portia, or mean-spirited home wreckers, like Arline. Whether good or evil, the women of soap operas were almost always more powerful than the male characters in the stories. "Every soap-opera heroine . . . is . . . a much stronger person than her husband or any man in her orbit," said Mona Kent.

In an interview with *Time* magazine in 1949, Mona Kent said she enjoyed writing for radio, but at times she felt "shame" at turning out such melodramatic stories. Whenever she attempted to write realism into the drama, however, her fans—or

Between 1940 and 1951, Mona Kent wrote all the episodes of the radio soap opera Portia Faces Life. *The cigarette-in-hand pose seems shocking to a modern reader who understands the dangers of smoking, but in the 1940s the media portrayed smoking as a desirable activity for the sophisticated woman.*

rather Portia's fans—sent an avalanche of angry letters to the radio station. Why? Did women believe Portia was a real-life person? At the

More Bad News

One of the first writers of radio soaps was Irna Phillips, a schoolteacher who left the classroom during the Depression to seek a career as an actress. Instead, she found fame and a profitable career as a writer of soap operas. The heroine of the radio soap opera *The Guiding Light* was Mary, the daughter of the Reverend Rutledge. Mary is to marry Ned, her childhood sweetheart, when suddenly Ned flees Five Points. But why has he abandoned sweet Mary? Reverend Ruthledge knows the answer. Ned's mother was a murderess! Such surprising bad news was sure to have shocked radio listeners. Ned eventually returns to Five Points. Mary is overjoyed, for she has never stopped loving him. But Ned brings with him some more bad news—his wife! Although she is crushed, Mary is not broken.

During the hard years of the Depression and later World War II, Irna Phillips earned thousands of dollars *a week* for writing her fifteen-minute radio scripts, filled with troubled characters, such as Mary and Ned, and conflicts that roiled with melodrama. Many American housewives loved the soaps. Perhaps by eavesdropping on other people's bad news, they might for a moment forget about their own hard luck.

beginning of each episode, the male radio announcer reminded listeners that this was a "story reflecting the courage, spirit, and integrity of American women everywhere." But did women listeners actually buy that line? Did they believe the dozens of soap opera stories that filled the daytime airwaves?

Probably not. Most women understood that Portia's character was made up and not real. Bad things happen to people, but how many bad things can happen to one person month after month, year after year? But that is exactly the point. Soap operas were serials, which means they continued day after day. To create suspense and tension, the female character needed to thwart her enemies—at least until the next problem arose. And so Portia allowed women to escape their reality for fifteen minutes a day. They loved Portia because she *wasn't* them. No doubt, more than a few women sighed at the end of each episode, relieved that her life wasn't nearly as bad as Portia's.

For fifteen minutes a day for eleven years, Portia faced the dramas of her life. In the final episode, Portia does not face an uncomplicated future, however. Convicted of a murder she did not commit, Portia goes to prison. Listeners—male as well as female—could only guess how she might get out of this tricky situation. Radio left Portia's fate to each listener's imagination.

The People's Palace

When the Christmas season of 1932 began, one out of every four workers did not have a job. And yet in New York City on December 27 of that year, floodlights crisscrossed the sky to announce the grand opening of "the people's palace." Wealthy industrialist John Rockefeller had originally intended to build a new opera house on the 12 acres (5 hectares) of land he owned in midtown Manhattan. Here divas from all over the world might sing their arias in Italian and German. The Great Depression changed his plans, but not his vision of grandeur. He formed a partnership with the Radio Corporation of America, and together they began construction on a complex of buildings, the heart of which would be a modern music hall. John D. Rockefeller intended Radio City Music Hall to be a place of inspiration and hope, as well as pleasure and entertainment.

Construction took years. When completed in 1932, Radio City Music Hall was the largest indoor theater in the world. Divas would still perform here, though. Operatic stars of popular music and dance and eventually of the moving pictures would also find a home here.

On opening night, socialites wrapped in furs stepped from their chauffeur-driven cars and entered the theater. The show that evening promised to be exciting, but even if the curtain never rose, the house itself was entertainment enough. A grand arch rose more than 100 feet (30 meters) high to frame the stage, which was itself 144 feet (44 m) long—about half the

Many well-to-do New Yorkers dressed in their finest to attend the grand opening of Radio City Music Hall in 1932.

length of a football field! The interior was a modern style of architecture called art deco. The walls and ceilings swept upward in curves that created a sense of immense space. The theater could seat nearly six thousand people. More than twenty-five thousand lights illuminated the hall. *Time* magazine marveled at the hall's technical innovations—the stage revolved, the floodlights could disappear, a hydraulic system allowed sets to rise upward or to lower out of sight, and an incredibly large Wurlitzer organ was built just for the theater. The organ's smallest pipe was just a few inches (centimeters) high, but its largest pipe measured 32 feet (10 m)!

Among the entertainers that first night were Rockefeller's intended opera stars, but there were also minstrel performers, comedians, even circus acts—including a high-wire performance. The Roxyettes also performed. This precision dance troupe featured sixteen showgirls, each remarkably alike in appearance. Their costumes revealed their stockinged legs. They performed their "eye-high" kicks in unison as if they were a single dancer. Radio City Music Hall on opening night was not their first performance. But the hall became their permanent home and they, too, gained a permanent name: the Rockettes.

The Rockettes perform at Radio City Music Hall in the 1930s.

Dancing for Dough

A dance marathon was a type of contest to challenge a couple's endurance. The partners danced and kept dancing for as long as they could stand, sometimes days, sometimes weeks. In the 1920s, dance marathons were an amusement, a crazy way of having fun and gaining fame or a place in the record books. Alma Cummings, an American woman, started the craze in the 1920s. She danced for twenty-seven hours without stopping. During those hours, she outlasted six male partners. Her physical feat made newspaper headlines. Soon other women and some men too tried to set new dance endurance records. In the 1930s, dance marathons became a way to earn much-needed dollars. Partners entered the contests with the hope of earning a cash prize as high as two thousand dollars. For many this fortune was worth the risk of swollen feet, dehydration, and physical exhaustion. Nurses were in attendance, and an ambulance carried away more than one dance partner. Even if a person didn't win the top prize, dance marathons provided shelter and food for a few days or weeks. The longest dance marathon during the Depression continued for more than five thousand hours!

Spectators came to the marathons to watch and sometimes cheer for their favorite couple. But marathons emphasized endurance rather than dancing ability. Many people objected to marathons as a health risk. Many contestants collapsed from exhaustion.

This woman in a Depression-era dance marathon is actually sleeping. But as long as her partner is able to hold her up, the pair can stay in the contest.

In the 1930s, the music of big bands was wildly popular. Musicians such as Duke Ellington, Count Basie, Woody Herman, Glen Miller, and Benny Goodman played a type of jazz music called swing. Not only did big bands and swing music help keep the music industry alive during the Great Depression, but they also help to bring joy and just plain good fun to Americans all across the country.

Usually a big band had fifteen to twenty musicians, sometimes more, playing horns as well as guitar, bass, and drums. The trumpets, trombones, clarinets, and saxophones gave swing music a brassy and bright sound. Swing could be sweet (meaning slow and mellow) or hot (meaning fast, loud, and brassy). The bands often featured soloists who crooned into the microphone. Soloists often stood offstage or sat in chairs to the side of the band during instrumental numbers. Soloists stood in the spotlight at the microphone to perform their solos. Often the crooner was a female. The women brought glamour and a bit of class to swing music and were one of the reasons for its great popularity.

Ella Fitzgerald got her big break as a female vocalist in Chick Webb's band in a most unexpected way. She was sixteen, and she had occasionally been in trouble with the police since the death of her mother a few years earlier. Her father had abandoned the family. On a May evening in 1934, she got the opportunity to perform at the Apollo Theater in New York's Harlem neighborhood during an amateur competition. The first-place prize was twenty-five dollars, and

Twenty-year-old Ella Fitzgerald, shown here in Asbury Park, New Jersey, in 1938, would be surprised to know that she was on her way to becoming the nation's most popular female jazz singer. In her lifetime, she would win thirteen Grammy Awards and sell more than 40 million albums.

Fitzgerald certainly needed the money. She had intended to dance in the competition. While waiting backstage, however, she became so nervous that when her turn came to perform, she couldn't move. The audience, she remembered, was laughing.

She decided to sing instead. And when she did, something magical happened. The audience had been rowdy, but now they listened in awe. And then they applauded her. They demanded she sing again and then again! From that moment in the spotlight, Ella Fitzgerald's life changed. She knew she wanted to sing forever. Chick Webb hired her, and her career as a female vocalist began. By 1938 her cheerful song "A-Tisket, A-Tasket" had sold one million copies.

Ethel Waters, Billie Holiday, Peggy Lee, and Helen Forrest were also popular singers with swing bands during the 1930s and 1940s, often in hotel ballrooms or nightclubs. The music of the big bands and their female vocalists, however, also played over the radio and on jukeboxes. A jukebox was a large record-playing machine, often lit up with bright, colorful lights. Nickels and

The Lindy Hop, known for its acrobatic aerial movements, began in New York's Harlem neighborhood and then spread across the United States, eventually becoming the basis for the jitterbug (shown above).

The term jukebox *was coined in the 1930s. The word possibly came from* jook, *the African American slang word for "dance." The machines (above) obtained their colorfully lighted, gaudily decorated look in the late forties, reflecting the festive atmosphere that came after the Great Depression and World War II were over.*

dimes dropped into the machine provided hours of dancing. A juke joint was anyplace where people got together to dance to the music in the jukebox.

Just as swing music was loud and brassy, so too were the swing dance movements. The Tutti-Frutti, the Big Apple, and especially the Lindy Hop, named after aviator hero Charles Lindbergh's 1927 solo flight (or hop) across the Atlantic, were among the most popular. Men and women who danced the Lindy Hop were acrobatic in their movements. They twisted and twirled around, and men lifted their female partners over their heads or swung them onto the floor between their legs.

The popularity of radio and jukeboxes was another reason for swing's popularity. People didn't have to dress up and go to a fancy ballroom to listen, dance, and have fun. For a few nickels, a guy and gal could forget their troubles on the dance floor wherever that dance floor was—in a ritzy nightclub, in a farmhouse kitchen while the radio played, or in a juke joint on Saturday night.

MRS. AMERICA
GOES TO THE MOVIES

chapter two

*The movies . . . were not necessarily telling women not to have careers;
they were telling them that their best choice of career was love—not
washing dishes, or cleaning house, or even having children . . . but love.
Over and over again the answer to the question of what a woman should
do with herself was wrapped in shiny paper and presented as love.*

—Jeanine Basinger, *A Woman's View: How Hollywood Spoke to Women 1930–1960* (1993)

The Filmmakers of the Motion Picture Industry

in 1930s' Hollywood were expert at creating fantasies, such as this one for its audiences: Fifty-four chorus girls in skimpy costumes made of large gold coins and seemingly nothing else, sing:

> We're in the money, we're in the money;
> We've got a lot of what it takes to get
>   along!
> We're in the money, that sky is sunny,
> Old Man Depression you are through,
>   you done us wrong.

The costume designer for the movie musical *Gold Diggers of 1933* reportedly required fifty-four thousand coins to create the costumes. For the people sitting in the movie theater, seeing all that gold glitter (not to mention the bare legs of beautiful chorus girls) was fun and well worth the nickels they had paid to see the movie. After the opening number ends, the character development and conflict begins. Three of the chorus girls, Carol, Trixie, and Polly, have lost their jobs. The song they have just rehearsed, "We're in the Money," has become a cruel irony. On the street with nowhere to go, they wonder where they will find their next meal. This would have struck a familiar chord with the audience, many of whom might have had a similar experience.

The Great Depression had slipped its fingers into the pockets of Americans everywhere. Although thousands of movie theaters closed and movie ticket sales declined, Hollywood was in the business of entertaining people. In 1933 sixty million people still went to the movies. Because so

Though the movie appeared to be pure escapism, Gold Diggers of 1933 *dealt with serious social themes. Shot during the Great Depression, the film's main characters are more worried about where their next meal is coming from than digging for gold. One of the film's songs, "Remember My Forgotten Man," is about the fate of veterans of World War I (1914–1918). The film also embraces FDR's social programs, such as the New Deal, and looks forward to a new era of prosperity.*

many of these moviegoers were women, the Hollywood studios created their celluloid fantasies with them in mind.

CHARACTERS AND CONFLICTS, CHOICES AND CONSEQUENCES

In the 1930s and 1940s, movies gave women and girls something glamorous to dream about. For a few hours in a darkened movie house, she could imagine what her life might be like if she were that character on the screen.

Women's movies—films made especially to attract female viewers—were about all kinds of interesting characters: shop girls, chorus girls, secretaries, heiresses, spinsters, misunderstood wives, widowed mothers trying desperately to care for their children, and fast-talking working women who barge into a man's world and demand to be taken seriously. More often than not, their stories unfolded in a variety of interior sets: living rooms, dining rooms, kitchens, offices, hotel suites, restaurants, and, of course, ballrooms. Few images showed women physically

By the late 1940s, advances in film technology—including sound, lighting, special effects, and the use of color—brought theater audience attendance to all-time highs. Young women were particularly attracted to the on-screen glamor of the ever-more elaborate productions.

active, scaling a mountain or flying an airplane. They wore beautiful clothes—gowns that trailed behind as they walked down staircases, well-tailored suits, and perky little hats. And the women in the audience could dream of owning such a house and dining in such a restaurant and wearing all those glamorous clothes.

Vivien Leigh portrayed the feisty Southern lady Scarlett O'Hara in Gone with the Wind *(1939). Hollywood heartthrob Clark Gable played the dashing Rhett Butler.*

Women's movies were also about choices and consequences. The plotlines usually focused on a decision a woman must make, often about whether to choose a career over love or which man to choose as a husband. In the 1939 film *Mr. Smith Goes to Washington*, for example, Clarissa Saunders is "one of the guys." The politicians and the journalists call her by her last name. She's feisty and witty. She is also very smart and teaches the naive senator everything he needs to know about how a bill becomes law. She is a secretary and not a congresswoman or senator. Her decision to help Senator Jefferson Smith expose the corrupt politicians in the Senate lands her Hollywood's greatest prize: a husband. As the movie ends, the women in the audience understand that Clarissa Saunders will soon become Mrs. Jefferson Smith.

Women who make the wrong choice, on the other hand, suffer. In the 1939 movie *Gone with the Wind*, tough, enterprising Scarlett O'Hara loves Ashley, but he loves sweet, saintly Melanie. Although Scarlett marries the dashing Rhett Butler, year after year she yearns for Ashley. When at last she discovers she really does love Rhett, he's had enough of her yearning after someone else. He leaves her. Scarlett sobs. She begs his forgiveness, but he gives her none.

"But what will happen to me?" she cries.

In one of film history's most memorable closing lines, Rhett Butler says, "Frankly, my dear, I don't give a damn." There was no happy ending for Scarlett. Filmmakers intended their female audiences to relate to the saintly Melanie and to scorn the selfish Scarlett. Many Mrs. Americas did just that.

Women's movies were also about contradictions, about breaking stereotypes but also enforcing them. Single women were lonely and longed for love. Married women were often unhappy. And, whether married or single, working women were smart as well as being lonely and unhappy. Their husbands could be devious and downright dishonest, falling in love with other women or getting so wrapped up in their work they forgot they even had wives waiting at home. In *The Bishop's Wife (1947)*, an angel comes down to Earth to cheer up the lonely wife of a bishop and to spark some jealousy in the husband. All ends well. The bishop realizes how much he loves his wife, and the angel returns to the clouds. And the women in the audience could dream that everything in their lives could also end well.

In The Bishop's Wife (1947), *the title character, played by Loretta Young, discovers a perfectly decorated Christmas tree in her parlor, courtesy of Cary Grant (left) in his role as her heavenly visitor.*

Screwball Comedies and Stereotypes

A screwball comedy was a very popular type of movie during the Great Depression. The name *screwball* comes from the baseball term for a fast but wild pitch that confuses the batter. In films the pitcher is usually a woman and her wild antics confuse the men in her life.

In *Bringing Up Baby* (1938), heiress Susan Vance decides she wants to marry a handsome but absentminded professor named David, who is reconstructing a dinosaur skeleton. Susan is a "madcap," which means someone, usually a girl, who is wildly impulsive and reckless. Susan has a pet leopard, Baby. Through a bit of conniving, she gets the professor to help her take the leopard to her farm in Connecticut. Her plan is to get the professor away long enough so that he'll fall in love with her and not marry Alice, the other woman in his life. "I'm gonna marry him," Susan tells her aunt. "He doesn't know it but I am."

Although the pet leopard gets lost and the professor ends up in jail, Susan's screwball pitch works. So do the stereotypes:

One: Women are illogical and scatterbrained. "You look at everything upside down," the professor tells Susan. "I've never known anyone quite like you."

Two: What women want more than anything is to fall in love and get married. At the end of the film, David realizes that the past few days spent with Susan were the most fun he's ever had in his life. He tells her he loves her. Minutes later, Susan—forever reckless—accidentally topples his dinosaur reconstruction, which had taken him four years to complete. As Susan climbs out from beneath the mountain of fossilized bones, she says sheepishly, "Oh look what I've done. Can you ever forgive me?"

Of course, he can. Men have been forgiving women's foolish behavior forever. And that is stereotype number three.

Katharine Hepburn (right) *played a screwball heiress in* Bringing Up Baby (1938), *but she was an intelligent and independent woman who challenged society's stereotypes.*

Pictured in front of the Capitol Theater on Broadway in New York is part of the crowd of ten thousand, mostly women and children, who surrounded the entire block to wait in line for the August 17, 1939, opening performance of the film The Wizard of Oz.

These contradictions could be confusing, at least they were for Jeanine Basinger when she was a child watching the films of the 1930s and 1940s. In one movie, the female characters might be afraid of spiders, recalls Basinger. But in another film, they were "completely capable of bopping villains on the heads with frying pans."

Basinger understood that the movies were fantasies, but she also gleaned a truth about these female characters that stuck with her long after she left the theater. The woman in the film may have flaws and make poor choices but, says Basinger, "she is not weak and she is not stupid. Men constantly have to cope with her. She can wreck their dinosaur models, outshoot them in a rifle contest, poison their mushrooms, and reduce them to gibbering idiots. She can, and she does." Take Dorothy, for example, the little girl from Kansas who accidentally kills one of the wicked witches in *The Wizard of Oz* (1939). She may be female and a child, but she has power she doesn't even know she has. The house falling on the Wicked Witch of the East was an accident, and throwing the water on the Wicked Witch of the West, causing her to melt, was a stroke of good luck. But throughout Dorothy's journey through Oz, no one rescues her. She saves herself.

Along the way, Dorothy makes choices that have positive consequences for others—the scarecrow, the tin man, and the lion. She boosts their self-esteem and their courage. She gets herself home by herself, no thanks to the wizard, whose bag of magical tricks is an empty sack.

"There's no place like home. There's no place like home," Dorothy repeats over and over. And this mantra is magic. When she wakes up, she is back in Kansas. This more conventional theme—that home is where Dorothy and other celluloid characters, especially the female ones, belong—is repeated in many films of the 1930s. Once the United States entered World War II in 1941, however, that theme would change.

"BOOP IN COURT"

Not all women characters in the movies were played by flesh-and-blood actresses. Betty Boop, for example, was a cartoon created by the Max Fleischer Studios. She started her life much the same way as Blondie had—as an inanimate cartoon drawing. Betty, however, was originally a French poodle and not a flapper. In the 1930s, Betty made the successful transition from the funny papers to motion pictures, from French poodle to woman.

In her first movie, *Dizzy Dishes* (1930), Betty Boop was a poodle singing in a night-club where her boyfriend, Bimbo the dog, worked as waiter and chef. In subsequent movies, Betty's long poodle ears morphed into dangling earrings and she became human . . . and controversial! As a woman

Betty Boop was among the first cartoon characters to display female sexuality. Her short skirt and garter revealed a female body. She also wiggled and rolled her big eyes.

rather than a dog, she wore a very short dress, usually strapless, and a garter around her thigh. Although Betty looked brazen and wiggled and giggled a lot, she was really a good girl. Men were always trying to spy on or chase her, but Betty never let anyone steal her "boop-oop-a-doop."

What exactly was "boop-oop-a-doop"? It was just a noise, but sung by Betty, it was something more: it was her charm, her innocence, her babyish cuteness. Both Betty and her boop-oop-a-doop became a cultural icon in the early 1930s.

boop-oop-a-doop!

President Roosevelt's 1932 presidential campaign was in full swing when Max Fleischer Studios released Betty's next big hit. This movie was a full-length feature film titled *Betty Boop for President*.

At the time, the premise of a woman running for president was very funny. After all, women had only won the right to vote in 1920. Betty's campaign promises, however, were right in line with American sentiments. If elected, Betty Boop would take from the rich and give to the poor. She ran against a stick figure called Mr. Nobody. His campaign song is pure political satire: "When you're hungry, who feeds you? Mr. No-body. Who cares what becomes of you? Mr. No-body."

Comedy works when people can laugh about what they fear. Betty Boop allowed them to do this. Not surprisingly, she wins the election! She goes to Congress and "pushes through a program of boop-oop-a-doop and chocolate ice cream." She initiates other improvements too, such as carpeting laid over potholes in the streets, horses that wear high-heeled shoes, and policemen who halt traffic so that cats and dogs can cross the street.

Betty's animated movies were popular cinema amusements. And yet, as a cultural icon, Betty triggered some political controversies that were quite real. In 1932 actress Helen Kane sued the Max Fleischer Studios for $250,000. The actress had been popular in the 1920s, but her Hollywood star was falling fast. In her lawsuit, she claimed the studio had stolen her trademark baby-doll appearance and "boop-oop-a-doop" phrase. In fact, Helen Kane did have an adorable round face, large eyes, and dark hair that she wore in spit curls against her forehead and cheeks—just like Betty Boop. And in the 1920s, she had a hit song titled "I Want to Be Loved by You." She ended each verse by singing, "boop-oop-a-doop."

It seemed that Helen Kane had a strong case. In the darkened courtroom, the actress's attorneys played recent Betty Boop cinema cartoons as well as one of Kane's films from the 1920s. The judge asked the actress to arrange her hair like the cartoon character so he could see the resemblance. Then Kane took the witness stand. "I have become a ghost," she told the courtroom. "Recently in Hollywood when some children ran to open the door of my car, they greeted me as Betty Boop."

Then the defense began to argue their case. The attorneys for Max Fleischer

Known as the "boop-oop-a-doop" girl, actress and singer Helen Kane believed she was the inspiration for the cartoon character Betty Boop.

brought into the courtroom three actresses who had played the "voice" of Betty Boop in the movies. Mae Questel, Margy Hines, and Bonnie Poe wore their hair in spit curls and they, too, sang in their babyish voices "boop-oop-a-doop."

In the end, the judge ruled against Helen Kane. Max Fleischer might have copied her act and even her mannerisms, but Helen Kane could not prove that her singing style was her own unique creation. The story made headlines in newsmagazines. One headline read: "BOOP IN COURT" as if Betty were a real person.

Betty would get in trouble again. The issue was public morality, and this time, Betty would lose.

THE HAYS CODE

The popularity of Betty Boop and other movies triggered concerns among community leaders of the 1930s. Moving images were so realistic, so *visual*, that some people believed they were dangerous. President Roosevelt stated that movies boosted morale during the hard times of the Great Depression. Yet religious and educational leaders feared that movies boosted an unhealthy interest in crime and in sexual relationships outside of marriage. They believed that images of movie gangsters who shot their way out of a bank could seed ideas of crime in the minds of would-be robbers, especially during the Depression years when so many had so little. Women wearing seemingly nothing but gold coins, as in *Gold Diggers of 1933*, could likewise seed immoral thoughts. These leaders felt that something had to be done.

The Motion Picture Producers and Distributors Association (MPPDA) was an organization of filmmaking studios, including Twentieth Century Fox, Paramount, Warner Brothers, and Metro-Goldwyn-Mayer. The organization produced a censorship code to guide what could and could not be shown and said on the silver screen. Some studios ignored the production code, however. They produced films with intentionally bawdy storylines and situations as well as violent crime scenes as a way to increase audience attendance, which had dropped during the Depression.

Then, in 1934, the situation changed. The Catholic Church established an organization called The Legion of Decency. The purpose of the legion was to pressure Hollywood studios to produce movies of high moral standards according to the teachings of the church. The legion screened films and then gave each film a rating of A, B, or C. A films were those that had nothing objectionable. B films were "objectionable in part." The film might contain a line or sequence of images "contrary to the teaching of the Church." C films were immoral and condemned.

As an arm of the Catholic Church, the Legion of Decency had a powerful influence. The legion threatened a national boycott of movies if the MPPDA did not begin enforcing its production code. During the boycott, people would stop going to the movies. A national boycott of the movies surely would have brought the filmmaking industry to its knees. The Catholic Church was not alone in its criticism of the movies. Other religious groups, as well as some educational organizations such as the Parent Teacher Association (PTA), were demanding that Hollywood clean up its act.

And so the MPPDA agreed to enforce its censorship code. Will H. Hays was the president of the organization at the time, and so the code became known as the Hays Code. The Hays Code had three guiding principles:

1. No picture shall be produced that will lower the moral standards of those who see it. Hence the sympathy of the audience should never be thrown to the side of crime, wrongdoing, evil, or sin.

2. Correct standards of life, subject only to the requirements of drama and entertainment, shall be presented.

3. Law, natural or human, shall not be ridiculed, nor shall sympathy be created for its violation.

Once put into effect, even cartoon characters had to conform to the moral standards of the Hays Code. And so, Betty Boop's clothing and behavior changed dramatically. Her dresses had sleeves, and the length of her skirt covered her pudgy thighs and fell well below her knees. Gone was the garter belt. Gone, too, were Betty's suggestive wiggles and storylines. Instead of running away from men who leered at her, Betty spent her time in more wholesome, motherly activities—such as babysitting her little nephew. The new Betty Boop just wasn't the same. Her popularity dropped. Like Helen Kane, on whom she had been created, Betty Boop's Hollywood star was falling fast. Betty made her last movie in 1939.

Hollywood called actress Rita Hayworth Ravishing Rita. But the Hays Code demanded that her navel be covered in this publicity photograph from 1941.

At the same time, the Hays Code helped to shoot to stardom an innocent curly-haired child actress and dancer named Shirley Temple. She first began singing and dancing in 1931, when she was just three years old. Throughout the decade of the 1930s, she made

more than forty films. Shirley Temple represented not only childhood innocence and clean, family fun but also happy times during the Depression. President Roosevelt reportedly stated, "As long as our country has Shirley Temple, we will be all right."

Shirley's outstanding characteristic was her curly hair. "I had 56 curls that had to be set every night," she said. While mothers curled their daughter's hair in the same type of sausage rolls, little Shirley wished she could have short, tousled hair like her real-life heroine, aviatrix Amelia Earhart. Earhart had once visited Shirley on a movie set and sneaked her some chewing gum, which the baby star was not allowed to have.

Shirley Temple was the top motion picture attraction for 1935, according to *Time* magazine. Just a few years earlier, before the Hays Code, the Hollywood star who

Shirley Temple was ranked as the top-grossing box office star in the United States for four years. Her incredible popularity spawned a number of product tie-ins, among them a line of girls' dresses and hair bows as well as Shirley Temple dolls costumed as characters from her movies.

had drawn the largest audiences was bawdy Mae West, known for her racy humor and buxom figure. Good had triumphed over naughty. At least, for the time being.

IMITATIONS OF LIFE

The career woman image so popular in radio and film in the 1930s and 1940s was more an idealistic than a realistic portrayal of women's lives. In 1930 approximately 775,000 women worked in offices as stenog-raphers, or typists. Although that may seem like a lot, almost two million women worked as servants, including cooks and waitresses, and another two million worked as laborers in factories. Their stories were rarely told. Often missing, too, from films, radio programs, comic strips, cartoons, and most advertisements of the 1930s were images of women of color: African American, Hispanic, Asian, and Native American women.

The movies portrayed career women as beautifully dressed and made-up office workers. This was not the reality for the majority of working women who worked at much more menial tasks.

Why? Three reasons: entertainment, profits, and society's prejudices.

Entertainment. Movies, as a creation of popular culture, reflect the values and biases of the society at the time. In the 1930s, the United States was a divided country. Throughout many southern states, an African American could not go to the same school, church, or restaurant as a white person. They could not sit in the same movie theater as white Americans or at least not on the same day. Often they had to enter through rear doors and sit in balcony seats. Some African American filmmakers in Hollywood, such as Oscar Micheaux, made movies specifically for African American audiences. These popular "race movies," as they were called, provided positive images of African Americans as well as work for actors of color. But they did not play in every theater or even in every city. The mainstream Hollywood movies usually did. And while a small number of African Americans starred in a movie, the roles offered to most of them were at best secondary and often demeaning: a cook, a maid, a mammy, or an otherwise uneducated or amusing character.

Profits. Hollywood movie studios lured into their movie houses a specific type of person. According to Margaret Farrand Thorp, that typical moviegoer was female, white, middle class (her husband likely earned a comfortable $1,500 a year or more), and lived in a city. These women and their husbands were most likely to have the extra money to purchase movie tickets. Studios, therefore, made most films to appeal to their life experiences.

Given the racist attitudes of his times, African American filmmaker Oscar Micheaux's accomplishments were extraordinary. He wrote, produced, and directed forty-four feature-length films, among them God's Step Children (1938), in which a light-skinned girl tries to find her way in both the black and white worlds.

THE YELLOW PERIL

Mistrust and hatred of Chinese Americans in the United States dated back to the 1880s. At that time, the U.S. Congress passed the Chinese Exclusion Act, putting an end to immigration of Chinese laborers into the country. Popular media and many politicians referred to the Chinese as the yellow peril. This was a reference to the perceived skin color of Asians. The Chinese Exclusion Act was supposed to be temporary, but in 1902, Congress made the act permanent. (It was later revoked.) The stereotyping, discrimination, and violence against Asian Americans continued mainly because many people did not understand and so feared their customs and way of dressing. People also believed that the Chinese were taking jobs from white Americans. And because a very small number of Chinese men formed gangs, or tongs, this too created fear. Media depictions were also responsible for promoting stereotypical images of the Chinese as sinister. Newspapers reported on tong warfare in the Chinatown section of cities such as San Francisco. Movies, too, promoted negative stereotypes. In the 1930s, films such as those about the evil doctor Fu Manchu were very popular among American moviegoers. In these films, the Chinese, both men and women, were the villains. By the end of the movie reel, they had been punished for their misdeeds.

Movies contributed to the negative stereotyping of Asian Americans. Dating back to the days of silent movie-making, the Chinese characters, both men and women, were portrayed as villains who were always punished by the end of the reel for their misdeeds. This scene is from The Flower of Doom *(1917).*

Prejudice. Prejudice influenced the perceptions people had of minorities. One perception—enhanced by media images—was that all African Americans lived in sharecroppers' shacks or crowded tenement (slum) buildings. Such impoverished settings didn't fit the formula for screwball comedies or melodramatic soap operas. Although these were the places in which many American women of all races lived and worked, movies were entertainment. Reports of real life with all of its hardship were better left to the newspapers and the glossy picture magazines, such as *Life* and *Look*.

The African American woman who went to the movies had a limited choice of what she'd see: films in which her image was missing from the screen entirely or films in which only stereotypical images of her race are seen. The same was true for Asian American, Hispanic American, and Native American women. The representation of women of color in the movies was neither real nor ideal. They were stereotypes.

In 1933 Fannie Hurst wrote a best-selling book called *Imitation of Life*. It told the story of two single mothers, Bea Pullman, who is white, and Delilah Johnson, who is black, struggling to make ends meet. Bea hatches a brilliant plan—she and Delilah will go into business together selling Bea's syrup and Delilah's secret family recipe for pancakes. The novel is about much more than just a career woman business venture. It explores the troubled relationships between the mothers and their daughters.

A year later, in the Hollywood film based on the novel, African American actresses Louise Beavers played Delilah, and Fredi Washington played her daughter, Peola. The film was controversial. First, in the 1930s, a white woman and black women going into business was most unusual. Second, the film dared to show a beautiful young black woman (Fredi) passing for a white woman. Peola is light skinned. People who don't know that her mother is Delilah mistake Peola for a white woman. "There is nothing wrong in passing," Peola argues with her mother. "The wrong is the world that makes it necessary."

That world was a segregated United States, a nation that in the 1930s discriminated against people of color. Moreover, in this world, there was something wrong about passing, at least according to the law books of many southern states, which made it illegal for members of different races to marry. In *Imitation of Life*, Peola leaves home and, passing as a white woman, marries a white man. To maintain her false identity, Peola disowns her mother. Even if Delilah sees her walking down the street, Peola instructs, her mother must not acknowledge her. "You mustn't see me, or own me, or claim me or anything," Peola tells her. "You'll have to pass me by."

Actress Louise Beavers (left) gave a powerful performance as the heartsick mother Delilah Johnson in the film Imitation of Life *(1934). Actress Claudette Colbert played Delilah's employer. Beavers would act in dozens of films and later, television programs, usually portraying a housekeeper, a cook, or a slave.*

Peola's betrayal, not only of her mother but of her race, results in Delilah's death . . . of a broken heart. At the funeral, Peola returns full of regret and sorrow. The audience understands that she has suffered. Peola will stop "passing" and accept her blackness.

The film was also controversial for reasons other than what the story was about. For perhaps the first time ever, a mainstream Hollywood film addressed the concerns of an African American mother. Delilah's character was a stereotype, but Louise Beavers's performance got some white women in the audience thinking. Was it possible that

African American mothers cared about the same things and experienced the same emotions that they did?

This film was no screwball comedy. *Imitation of Life* was a melodrama intended to wring buckets of tears from the eyes of the audience. And it did! But people cried for different reasons. Mrs. White America might have cried because of the tragedy of Delilah's life. How bitter to have a daughter so ungrateful and so uncaring. Some African American women, such as feminist scholar and writer bell hooks, cried for Peola. Hooks claimed that *Imitation of Life* changed *her* life for a while. Faced with the unpleasant choice of choosing between no image of her real self on the screen and images that made sweeping generalizations about all black women, she'd rather not go to the movies at all. And so she didn't for a very long time.

An interesting footnote to this story concerns the talented actress Fredi Washington. In real life, Washington was light skinned and had green eyes. Her resemblance to her screen character Peola ended there, however. Despite her powerful performance in *Imitation of Life*, she found additional Hollywood roles difficult to get. The color of her skin was much too light to secure her roles as an African American woman. When she did get those roles, the costume and makeup artists darkened her skin with cosmetics. Some Hollywood producers encouraged Washington to "pass for white" as a way to get more leading roles. Unlike the fictional Peola, Fredi Washington was immensely proud of her race and absolutely refused.

Frosted Yellow Willows

"Every time your picture is taken, you lose a part of your soul," Sam Wong told his daughter. He had just learned that she was often absent from school in the afternoons to play a small role in a Hollywood movie. He was angry. His disobedient daughter was disgracing his family. Anna May Wong was just fourteen, but already she knew she wanted to become a star of the silver screen. Her father had other ideas for his daughter. She would follow the traditional Chinese ways. She would marry and become a dutiful wife, as her mother had done.

Anna May Wong was a third-generation Chinese American. Her grandparents had lived in the Chinatown neighborhood of Los Angeles, California, and there, too, her parents were born. Anna May was born in 1905 in a section of Los Angeles just beyond Chinatown. Her parents named her Wong Liu Tsong, meaning "Frosted Yellow Willows." Although her parents were U.S. citizens, they strongly believed in the traditional Chinese ways. Among these was the belief that a good girl does not become an actress. In Sam Wong's eyes, an actress was no different from a courtesan, or prostitute. Anna May saw things differently. She was a modern California girl. When a movie crew came to Chinatown to film, she was often among the spectators in the streets. She risked a whipping with a bamboo stick by her father, but the glamour of the silver screen was worth it. "I would worm my way through the crowd and get as close to the cameras as I dared," she remembered.

Despite her father's disapproval, Wong continued to make movies. At seventeen she was unusually tall for a woman of her race, measuring 5 feet 7 inches (170 cm). Her eyes, too, were unusually large. Although these two characteristics were not particularly prized among Chinese people, they were Wong's passport to fame on the silent silver screen. At first, her roles were minor, but she felt as if the cameras were looking only at her. Still, her father protested. The cameras looked at her only when they needed an Asian girl, and the only Asian girls Hollywood wanted were to play the roles of courtesans, thieves, and villains.

In time, Wong came to understand how right her father was. Despite her talent, the roles Hollywood writers scripted for her were pure stereotypes. She played the beautiful but evil "dragon lady." She almost always died, a fitting end for her evil characters. Often, in shame, her character committed suicide. While at first, she had accepted these roles, by the mid-1920s, she had tired of being typecast. She left the United States for Europe, where filmmakers and movie fans recognized the scope of her talent.

Anna May Wong was the first Chinese American actress to win international acclaim. Although she fought for other roles, directors cast her most often as a villainess.

By the 1930s, she had returned to America as an international star. Yet the scripts available for a Chinese American actress had changed very little. But there was one role Wong wanted very badly. A few years earlier, Pearl S. Buck had written a best-selling novel called *The Good Earth*. The novel presented, for perhaps the first time, a sympathetic portrait of ordinary Chinese Americans. The character O-lan and her husband Wang Lung had many of the same desires that other Americans had, including the need to provide a good home for their children. MGM Studios had purchased the movie rights to the novel. Wong wanted to play the role of the obedient O-lan. The studio was against it. She had played so many evil dragon ladies and seductive "China dolls" that they feared audiences would not accept her as the honorable O-lan. Officials representing the Chinese government also spoke against her. In China, they said, Anna May Wong was greatly disliked for accepting roles that were demeaning to Chinese women.

The only other role available to Anna May Wong was to play the role of the story's courtesan, Lotus. Some fan magazines at the time suggested that she turned down the role because she was insulted that Hollywood was hiring white actors to play the Chinese characters. Others rumored that MGM thought her too old and not beautiful enough to play Lotus. Wong's disappointment was huge. No

> *"A lot of people, when they first meet me, are surprised that I speak and write English without difficulty. But why shouldn't I? I was born in Los Angeles."*
>
> —Anna May Wong, 1926

The studios cast Paul Muni, a white actor, in the role of Wang Lung. That shut the door on Wong. As an Asian American, she could not play the wife of a white actor. It mattered not at all that Wong was American or that Paul Muni would act in "yellowface," a type of makeup to suggest he was Chinese. Movie production codes in 1936 reflected the prejudices of the times. Mixed races could not play opposite one another in roles that suggested they were married.

doubt, the words of her father had come back to haunt her. She decided to leave the United States once again, this time to travel to China, the country of her great-grandparents. But here, too, she met with disapproval. Chinese media criticized her for the roles she had agreed to play, not understanding that they were the only roles U.S. filmmakers had allowed her to play. *Movietone News* in Shanghai referred to her as a "puppet," and one newspaper called her "that stooge that disgraces China."

The MGM studio claimed that there were not enough Chinese actors to cast the movie The Good Earth *(1937). And the Chinese government threatened to ban the movie if any Japanese actors were used, as the second Sino-Japanese War was in progress. Thus new makeup techniques were developed specifically for the film, and Western actors Paul Muni* (left) *and Luise Rainer* (right) *played the lead roles.*

Anna May Wong was hurt, but she had faced racial discrimination all her life, and once again, in China, she rose above it. The trip to her grandparent's homeland was among the best experiences of her life, she told reporters. The nine months she spent in China had changed her, she said. She returned with "a deeper conviction" to make the world a better place and specifically to promote racial tolerance for her adopted country of China. She still acted in stereo-typical roles, for those were all that Hollywood had to offer her. But she had found a new mission in her life. A few months after her return to the United States in 1937, the armies of Emperor Hirohito of Japan invaded China. Anna May Wong actively raised money to send medical supplies to China to help war refugees. She worked with the American Red Cross and with other actors to raise awareness of China's great need in time of war.

chapter three
fashion's passions

just what is the condition of your costumes for your morning household duties? Do you have a neat little scrubbing costume? Or a nimble outfit for climbing ladders? Or are you the kind who serves breakfast attired in a limp, faded rag so your family will feel sorry for you because you have to stay home and work? Brace up, give your family a treat; send them off to a good day by buying, making or getting somehow a supply of new, gaily colored costumes for morning.

—Ladies' Home Journal, May 1936

each generation develops its own idea of what is beautiful.

During the nineteenth century, a woman's beauty bloomed from the good deeds she performed. Character and virtue were more important than the color of her eyes or the shape of her lips. That does not mean women weren't aware of their physical bodies or of popular fashions. Indeed, they were. The popular hoop skirt in the mid-nineteenth century involved tying a sort of cage around a woman's waist so that, once dressed, her extended hips made her waist seem small. Ladies of high society wore hoop skirts, and so did ordinary working women, such as parlor maids, seamstresses, and housewives. Likewise, to erase wrinkles, women of an earlier century boiled eggs into a paste to apply as a facial mask or wrapped their faces overnight in brown paper that had been soaked in vinegar. Some massaged the forehead and cheeks with a curious invention called the Electric Wrinkle Roller. It looked like a tiny rolling pin with a handle.

In the early decades of the twentieth century, however, society's concept of beauty shifted from the inside to the outside, from who a woman was to how a woman looked. Honor, purity, and faithfulness were still important qualities, but hair, eyes, skin, lips, hands, and weight became critical points for judging a woman. Lipstick, mascara, and nail polish—which had once been the signs of a woman with low morals—became socially acceptable in the 1920s. The rising popularity of movies was one reason. Women imitated the movie cosmetics of their favorite Hollywood stars. Other cultural factors contributed to the change as well, including women's growing independence as citizens and wage earners. Women had won the right to vote and were leaving their homes to work in public places. For some women, cosmetics were a way of expressing their individuality and their independence.

By the 1930s, mass advertisements on radio and in magazines persuaded women to purchase cosmetic products by appealing to her fear of growing old or being rejected by social acquaintances. You are being watched! these advertisements warned. Your husband, your friends, your employer . . . each is judging you by your appearance. For example:

"I'm convinced we wives grow careless—that husbands watch our complexions much more than we think . . . that look of youth is what men seek."
—Palmolive soap ad, *Woman's Home Companion*, 1932

The allure of Hollywood glamour inspired women's cosmetics as well as hair styles and clothing. The point of all this allure was to find—or keep—a man.

> "*i'm convinced we wives grow careless— that husbands watch our complexions much more than we think....*"
>
> —Palmolive soap ad, 1932

"His eyes don't stray to other faces since I took my beauty expert's advice." —Palmolive soap ad, *Ladies' Home Journal*, 1932

"Maybe you <u>are</u> pretty.... Prettiness isn't enough nowadays. <u>Dramatize</u> your interesting features. Make your face vivacious, interesting, youthful." —Dorothy Gray, *Harper's Bazaar*, 1936

The purpose of wearing cosmetics had changed. Instead of pleasing yourself, you must please others, as this advertisement from Coty suggests: "A lipstick . . . has one purpose in its brief and vivid life: to leave a lady's lips more alluring. What good is it if it doesn't?" To keep her husband faithful and to win the admiration of friends and business acquaintances, a woman must look closely at herself in the mirror. Cosmetics were no longer a choice but a necessity. Even during the Depression, when other businesses were losing profits or going bankrupt, cosmetic sales continued to climb.

The Short Skirt Versus Long Skirt Debate

The fashion fad of the 1920s was the flapper's boyish dress: straight lines that suggested women had no breasts or waists, and short skirts to just below the knee. "We thought ourselves charming," stated a fashion editor for *Vogue*. But with a new decade came new fashions and new attitudes. The fashion editors forgot about the styles of yesteryear. "Farewell straight lines," she writes.

Skirt lengths dropped dramatically during the decade of the Great Depression. The new style covered a woman's legs and emphasized instead her waist and ankles. Some men complained. "You were so much nicer with your short little skirts," said one.

Some women complained too—at least initially. On the campus of Hunter College in New York City, thousands of female students completed a poll conducted by the school's Journalism Club. The question was: do you like long skirts? Seventy percent of the women polled answered no. The skirts were "impracticable, uncomfortable and uneconomical," they said. Long skirts were "a step backward in the progress of woman's emancipation." The other 30 percent, however, voted yes. Short skirts, they argued, "had robbed women of their most fascinating attribute—mystery."

The debate was not limited to young women on college campuses. In New York City, a convention of doctors of osteopathic medicine discussed the health benefits of short skirts and low necklines. "Many people have told us how much more ultra-violet light direct from the sun can reach a woman's body when she is normally and sensibly dressed," said Dr. R. Kendrick Smith. "How could a woman stand as she ought to stand with a great weight of useless clothing hanging from her? How could she walk as God meant her to walk with a hobbling, crippling impediment of dry goods dragging at her feet and ankles?" (Of course, his argument in favor of ultraviolet radiation did not take into consideration recent medical research linking ultraviolet rays to skin cancer.)

> "*a* step backward in the progress of woman's emancipation."
> —a 1929 Hunter College poll of skirt lengths

And still, the debate continued. Actress Gertrude Lawrence addressed the members of the New York State Federation of Women's Clubs. Long skirts were feminine, she argued. "And every woman knows that the way to get things she wants is to be feminine and her husband will let her have her own way."

In the end, neither the college polls, the medical endorsements, nor the discussions at the women's clubs had much effect on the fashions of the 1930s. Once the young debutantes being formally presented to society and the Hollywood actresses began to wear the new styles, the debate ended. The fashion parade moved forward, in long skirts and high necks. Eventually, the majority of women would fall in line behind them.

Fashion of the early 1930s began to move away from the flapper styles of the twenties and take on a softer, more traditionally feminine look as waistlines moved upward to the woman's natural waist (left). *However, the Great Depression called for thrift, and thus keeping up with fashion often meant sewing one's own clothes. World War II was the major influence on fashions of the 1940s. The War Production Board regulated the industry, including the amount of fabric used in garments. As a result, styles became more tailored* (right), *with shorter, straighter skirts and cropped jackets.*

Keeping Up Appearances

"How's your breath today?" The question ran in large, bold letters across the top of full-page advertisements in a number of major magazines in the mid-1930s. An illustration showed a man in a tuxedo with his arms around a woman in an evening gown. He seems about to kiss her. Apparently, her breath is just fine. But the text warns the reader, yours might not be!

Smart Women—
The Debutante and the Girl Next Door

Vogue magazine warned its readers in the 1930s to beware of the "rippling tummy." Never buy a bathing suit that is too small. When trying on a bathing suit, a woman should (a) remove her girdle, (b) remove her high-heeled shoes, and (c) look over her shoulder at her backside in the mirror. Why? Others would be looking at her just as closely. A bathing suit was not just for swimming, after all.

The women who read *Vogue* apparently had plenty of leisure time to enjoy sunbathing, either at West Palm Beach in Florida or along a grassy riverbank in the Connecticut countryside. Fashion advertisements and articles that appeared in *Vogue* suggested hard times weren't terribly hard after all. An article on which gloves to wear emphasized the variety of social outings a *Vogue* woman attended, even during the Depression years. Like all fashions, gloves came with a set of rules that "smart" women followed:

"Smart women wear them at the opera. . . . At formal dances, a fair number of gloves are in evidence and are especially popular with debutantes. They are worn occasionally to dinners, but are removed when dinner is served. Pink-beige gloves of medium length, without buttons, are by far the smartest. . . . Daytime gloves are longer, covering the cuff or meeting the sleeves of the new shorter sleeved dresses. Short, stitched gloves fastening with one button are smart for sports."

Fashion's command also included silk stockings. A "smart" woman did not wear just any color of stocking. She matched her stockings to her face powder. "Sunplexion" was a type of stocking created by Madame Helena Rubinstein. The color was "keyed perfectly to match fashionable 'outdoor' complexions."

Of course, not every woman who read *Vogue* magazine was a debutante or socialite. Even so, the girl next door was likely to get her fashion ideas from a very different publication, the Sears® catalog. The Sears® language differed from the Vogue language, but the message from both was the same: the importance of being fashionable.

In 1934 Sears® advertised its catalog as "the thrift book of the nation." The catalog acknowledged the economic woes many Americans were suffering. "Reckless spending is a thing of the past," stated the autumn 1930 edition. Each page showed multiple images of women, children, and even men wearing Sears®'s version of "smart" fashions. *Smart*, in this case, meant "practical and affordable" as well as "stylish." Product descriptions did not

Inside the advertisement image:

Smash Values! Newest Styles in Guaranteed Washfast Shantung Type Poplin

Poplin DRESS SALE

- Gay New Prints
- Becoming Styles
- Generous Cut
- Neat-Looking Details
- Finer Quality Fabric
- Sturdy Stitching

SALE ENDS FEBRUARY 28th

79¢ Ea. Usually Sold at **$1.00**

These one-dollar dresses from Sears® were indeed, "Smart Values!" at seventy-nine cents each. Yet despite the low price, fashionable touches abound, including the newly popular nautical look and ultrafeminine shoulder ruffles.

mention the opera or the polo grounds. The price of each item, however, appears in large, bold type.

Vogue glowed over romantic ruffles. The Sears® catalog, too, praised clothing that suggested femininity and romance. A catalogue illustration showed models wearing evening dresses with ruffles over the shoulders and told its readers that their favorite actresses wore dresses just like these. Both *Vogue* and Sears® recommend the same laundering product, "gentle Lux," for keeping the clothes looking their best.

A full-page advertisement in *Vogue* for Natural Bridge Shoes emphasizes style, comfort (a "veritable day-long beauty treatment"), and value. In 1940 a pair cost $5.00 to $6.00. The Sears® catalog of 1939 offers shoes, as well, at $1.98 a pair. A debutante or the girl next door could get two pairs for the price of one. It just depended on whether the lady was a "smart" shopper.

Vogue was a fashion magazine. Sears® was a merchandise catalog. One had glossy photographs, articles, and paid advertisements; the other was "a department store in a book." Both had text and visual displays, and both had loyal readers. A comparison of the two publications highlights class distinctions among women in the United States during the 1930s. And yet, whether a socialite, working girl, or housewife, these women shared something in common: an interest in fashion.

Halitosis, or "unpleasant breath," as the ad states in parentheses, would "keep you out of things . . . mar friendship . . . kills off a romance . . . or jeopardize a business chance."

Play it "safe," the text advised. "Use Listerine." Fashion is all about appearances and presentation. But fashion is not only the cosmetics and hygiene products a woman uses or the style of clothes she wears. It also impacts how she keeps her home and cares for family, how she entertains, and how she spends her leisure time. For the middle-class wife of the 1930s, her house and her involvement in the community reflected her social standing and her husband's success in the business world.

If most people weren't rich in the 1930s, at least they could *look* rich. Diamonds made of cut glass glittered almost like the real thing. Even the wealthy wore them. A suntanned body also suggested prosperity and good health. Wealthy people vacationed in sunny places, such as Florida, which was fast becoming a winter playground for the upper classes. They had leisure time to play tennis or swim. Elizabeth Arden developed a cream that gave the skin a bronzed glow, as if a woman had sunbathed.

But even if a woman couldn't look prosperous with glass diamonds and artificially bronzed skin, she could at least make efforts not to appear down and out. Women's magazines in the 1930s frowned upon "domestic hands" and "worry lines" around the eyes. Shabby clothing, too, was a sign that a woman simply wasn't taking proper care of herself. The words *Great Depression* did not

Impeccable fashion sense, the best beauty products, and even mouthwash are presented as a path to the altar in advertisements. In this 1930s ad for mouthwash, "poor Elinor" bears the "stigma of halitosis."

appear specifically, at least not often. But keeping up appearances while making do with less was a serious theme frequently discussed.

The March 1932 issue of *Ladies' Home Journal* featured a color photograph of a luncheon table. "Nothing on this table cost more than ten cents," reads the text. The editors assured their readers that they could prepare a wonderful luncheon for eight people for just five dollars. One recipe required only a can of peas, a can of cream of mushroom soup, chopped parsley, and a sprinkle of American cheese, all baked in a casserole dish.

Advertisements, also, emphasized thrift. "You use canned food. Of course, every smart, modern housewife does," read one advertisement in *Ladies' Home Journal* from 1933. "There is no waste in

"*You use canned food.*

     Of course, every smart, modern housewife does."

—ad in *Ladies' Home Journal*, 1933

canned foods." Crisco, a shortening used for cooking, ran an advertisement with this teasing headline: "He'll never guess they're leftovers." The text warned wives that husbands look "scornfully at cold meat and warmed up vegetables."

Husbands, apparently, also controlled the household money. An advertisement for the American Telephone & Telegraph Corporation in the December 1933 issue of *Vanity Fair* showed a housewife talking to her workingman husband, who is attempting to read a newspaper. "One of the things I do want for Christmas is a TELEPHONE RIGHT HERE," she says, pointing to a table. The advertisement stressed that Christmas 1933 was no time to spend money on sentimental gifts. An extension telephone, on the other hand, was practical. Although a housewife managed the home, the message implies that she still needed the man's approval before spending *his* money.

Money was a serious topic, and the magazine writers gave women advice freely. Some articles taught women about the law. A husband was responsible for his wife's debts, even though he might not have agreed to her purchases, one article informed the readers. Another cautioned women not to give in to the temptation to buy whatever pretty dress or shoes caught their fancy.

"The modern woman asks what she can buy and if the answer is she can't buy what she wants, she gets along without it. Or she

"Are you as poor as you think you are?" asked Samuel Crowther in the March 1932 *Ladies' Home Journal*. His article scolded women who were miserly with their money. "The woman who boasts that she is not buying any new clothing at present prices is interpreting thrift in entirely the wrong way—and will regret it later." It was up to the woman to seduce her husband, likewise, to dress well. His job and the family's future might depend upon it.

Often the advertisements read like an

> "the woman who boasts that she is not buying any new clothing at present prices is interpreting thrift in entirely the wrong way—and will regret it later."
>
> —Samuel Crowther, 1932

discovers she can get something free that suits her just as well," wrote Margaret Culkin Banning. Be creative was the message. And yet at the same time and often in the same publication, articles and advertisements encouraged women to spend money. Purchases of clothing and household and beauty products were not luxuries, the writers emphasized. They were necessities. "One thing a man doesn't understand," wrote Banning, "is that a woman who runs a home has a constant burden of replacements, of little things to buy."

article or a short story. An advertisement for Ivory Soap, for example, features two girlfriends, Millie and Frances, who are talking over lunch. Frances, the text reads, looks charming in her lovely Paris clothes. Millie's clothing is not described, but her hands are.

"'Tom has done very well,'" Millie says, speaking of her husband's career.

"Just then Frances's eyes fell to Millie's hands resting on the white tablecloth. Her hands look, Millie knows, rough and scrubby. They don't look like the hands of a successful man's wife."

The Swimmer and the Bathing Beauties

As a girl growing up in the early 1900s, Crystal Eastman wanted to be a swimmer like her father. Women's bathing costumes, however, were cumbersome. The long skirt, the cotton stockings, and even the shoes were heavy in the water and restricted a woman's ability to swim. Crystal Eastman called herself a rebel. She cast off the old-fashioned bathing costume and wore instead "a man's suit," one with legs rather than a skirt. The suit revealed her "brown legs for all the world to see," she said, which both "startled and embarrassed her father."

The mannish one-piece bathing suits of the 1920s not only revealed a woman's legs but also her arms and a good deal of her neck. Many of the women who dared to wear these new costumes were not swimmers like Crystal Eastman. They wore the costumes to show off their bodies. For some, the revealing suits were an expression of their independence and freedom from old-fashioned ideas of modesty. Outraged, many religious and community groups condemned the bathing costumes. In Chicago, police arrested and even dragged scantily clad bathing beauties from the public beaches. Still, women persisted in challenging the old ways and eventually changed them.

By the end of the decade, a woman wearing a one-piece bathing suit was considered modern rather than immoral. In the 1930s, the style changed once again. *Vogue* even encouraged its female readers to purchase the latest style in bathing costumes—a two-piece suit that revealed a woman's skin above her waist, the midriff. "Go bare-waisted on the sunniest, laziest days," the magazine advised, then added, "Provided, of course, you have a sleek, flat midriff."

The most daring (and slim-figured) swimmer might have appeared in public in a two-piece bathing suit, but these 1937 Sears® catalog suits were stylish and revealing enough for most women.

How embarrassing for Millie! Was she telling the truth about Tom or trying to impress her friend with a little fib? Whether or not Tom was successful isn't the point. Millie's appearance, however, is.

Sports and Femininity

"Who am I? Who do I want to be?" Young women who asked themselves these questions in the 1930s and 1940s often found the answer in the pages of magazines and in the fictional stories they listened to on the radio or watched in movie theaters. The choices were limited by what society valued . . . or did not value.

A woman might aspire to be a "glamour girl," such as the debutantes whose photographs appeared in newspapers. In 1938 Mrs. Frederic N. Watriss introduced her seventeen-year-old daughter Brenda Frazier to "polite society" at a party held in the Main Ball Room of the Ritz-Carlton Hotel in New York City with more than one thousand guests attending. For months afterward, the press followed Brenda, speculating on which eligible bachelor the "deb" might bring to her next dance or charity benefit. When she appeared in society wearing a strapless gown, she started a new fashion passion across the country.

For some women, however, their passion was sports, not fashion. They were athletes serious about their sport. They didn't play games for leisure. They didn't wear strapless gowns or worry about petal-soft complexions. Because they didn't, 1930s society viewed them with suspicion. Ice-skating was tolerated, because it was graceful and pretty. A skater glided and twirled. While she might sometimes leap, she didn't tackle or jab an opponent. Long-distance swimming had also become more acceptable ever since nineteen-year-old Gertrude Ederle had stunned the world in 1926 by swimming the English Channel from France to England in fourteen hours and thirty-one minutes. The British press had written that women did not have the physical stamina

Heiress Brenda Frazier's December 1938 debutante party received so much publicity that her image made the cover of Life *magazine. The press's interest in the young woman was apparently encouraged by her mother who, Brenda (left) later claimed, had Brenda's tendons made longer in a painful operation so that she could wear higher heels for the event. Gertrude Ederle (right), on the other hand, stretched her own tendons as she rigorously trained for her 1926 record-breaking swim across the English Channel.*

for demanding sports and could never compete on the same level as a man. Ederle's grueling swim across the channel through crosscurrents and pummeling rain proved that assumption false. When her feet touched the sand on the English shore, she discovered she had beaten the best men's record for swimming the channel by two hours.

When Ederle returned home, Americans treated her as a hero with a ticker-tape parade through New York City. "Gertrude is just a plain home girl," her mother told *Time* magazine. "She does not smoke or drink. She does not go out with young men, except just once in a while."

Could a woman play as strong a game as a man? Many sportswriters suggested a woman could not. Even so, tennis champion Alice Marble impressed the sports world with her aggressiveness on the court. Society excused the characteristic, perceived as unfeminine, probably because Marble had more than just a powerful serve and forehand. She was pretty. A 1944 press release described her as "Slim, tanned a golden-brown and crowned with soft golden hair. She looked more like a movie star, not an athlete."

Yet even pretty Alice Marble couldn't convince journalist Jack Miley that athletic women were attractive. "A woman's place is in the home, and I never saw a girl yet who didn't look a sight better with a frying

A montage of photographs demonstrates Alice Marble's serve and backhand as she plays tennis at Forest Hills in New York in 1937. Teased by sportswriters because she was so attractive, Marble was someone to be taken seriously. She won eighteen Grand Slam championships from 1936 through 1940 and served as a spy during World War II.

pan than a tennis racquet," he wrote in the *New York Post*. "A female flushed face over a hot stove is not only prettier but more practical than a purple face produced by puffing and panting from participation in some masculine sport for which nature never intended her."

The way nature intended. This was the same argument the British press had used when writing about Gertrude Ederle's attempt to swim the English Channel. Sportswriter Paul Gallico used the same reasoning when arguing against girl athletes in an article in *Vogue* magazine. "I find it a bore, most of the time, to be superior and muscular and wear pants and be smart and decisive, frank and essentially honest," he wrote. These were characteristics that men had, but women did not. But, he reasoned, it wasn't their fault. Nature had made men one way and women another. Just as some doctors had debated the medical benefits of short versus long skirts, they argued that "girls aping the activities of boys" was not only unnatural, it might prove harmful, preventing them one day from having children.

Paul Gallico believed that truly feminine women did not want to be sports heroes or champions. What they really wanted was a husband. "You are not trying to tell me that you spend three hours in a beauty parlour, stifling under mud packs, roasting under driers, and getting tweezed, slapped, prodded, yanked, and waved just because you like it, are you?" he asked. No, he concluded women made themselves attractive for one reason only—to impress a man. He had advice for them. Stop sweating and getting all breathless.

Was he being sarcastic or serious? Readers apparently thought he was serious. After the article appeared in *Vogue*, he received a landslide of mail from angry female readers. The letters sent Mr. Gallico essentially the same message: "Don't flatter yourself. . . . Girls do not make themselves attractive for men. And men look pretty awful, too, all 'mussed' and 'perspiring' and 'red-faced.'"

> "*a woman's place is in the home, and I never saw a girl yet who didn't look a sight better with a frying pan than a tennis racquet.*"
>
> —Journalist Jack Miley, 1944

Tennis Slurs, Anyone?

In the 1930s, women's tennis suddenly found ink on the sports pages of national magazines. This new attention came, in part, to a new emphasis on physical fitness for women and to the exciting victories of U.S. tennis stars: Helen Hull Jacobs, Alice Marble, and Helen Wills Moody. In an article on Alice Marble, *Time* described her as a "good-natured, green-eyed Tomboy" who could "hit a tennis ball like a man, and nearly as hard."

The sportswriters for *Time* tended to tack adjectives to athlete's names. For example, when writing about the male tennis players, the sportswriters most often used phrases such as these: defending champion Donald Budge, Budapest-born Gene Mako, or black-haired Francis Xavier Shields. On the other hand, in an article titled "Thick and Thin," *Time* magazine's sportswriter described Betty Nuthall as "stocky and thick-waisted" and her opponent Dorothy Round as "thin, plain." Given the title of the article, the sportswriter might have been having a little fun with words by commenting on the contrasting size of the women. Other articles, however, contain similar unflattering word choices: "husky" Nancy Wynne, "chubby, fat-legged" Dorothy May Sutton Bundy, "twinkled-toed" Sarah Palfrey Fabyan, "saucy, snub-nosed" Peggy Scriven, "leathery oldster" Molla Mallory, and "hefty" Jaja Jedrzejowska. Jaja, by the way, was a typist from Poland, the magazine reported, whose "powerful forehand had been strengthened by beefsteak breakfasts."

The sportswriters believed that their readers were interested in or at least amused by these descriptions of the female players. A few descriptions scattered here and there are amusing, but taken all together, an attitude begins to emerge from the sports pages: Women who compete, even in a pretty sport such as tennis, are tomboys or worse . . . muscle-bound Amazons who rejected men altogether.

Molla Mallory (above) *won a record-breaking eighth U.S. singles Championship in 1926 at the age of forty-two. Helen Wills Moody did not lose a set between 1927 and 1932. She is pictured below winning the Wimbledon Women's Singles title in 1930.*

Paul Gallico couldn't be swayed. "I want all you girls, whether you are athletes or not, to look beautiful, cool, calm . . . with your hair in order and decently brushed *all* the time." No amount of letters from angry women would change his mind.

The Muscle Moll

Mildred "Babe" Didrikson was no Alice Marble. She wasn't pretty, nor were the sports in which she competed. A woman who leaped hurdles or threw a javelin on the track field was considered vulgar. She had to spread and stretch her legs to clear the hurdle and twist

At the age of twenty-one, Babe Didrikson competed in three events at the 1932 Olympics—only because women were not allowed to enter more than three. She easily won the javelin event with a hurl of 143 feet 4 inches (43.5 m). Then she broke the world record in the 8-meter hurdles and tied for silver in the high jump.

her torso to launch the javelin. A woman who excelled and even beat a man at these activities was a "muscle moll." The phrase was unflattering. A *moll* was a slang term for "a woman gangster." Rough, uncouth, and a lawbreaker, a moll wasn't a lady.

Didrikson was tough and a braggart to boot. She intimidated her opponents. "Ah'm goin' whup all ya," she'd threatened them in her Texas drawl and then go ahead and do just that. In 1932 she won two gold and one silver medal in track-and-field competition during the Olympic Games. She was just nineteen. She excelled at other sports too, including basketball and baseball. She wrestled, lifted weights, bowled, and shot pool. Billiards are played by using a long stick to knock colorful balls into the pockets of a pool table. Pool halls, however, were dark, smoky rooms frequented by men mostly. Babe probably wasn't afraid to go into those kinds of places. She could take care of herself. After all, she could lift a 50-pound (23 kg) weight over her head.

The popular media of the 1930s loved pinning labels on U.S. sports stars. Babe Ruth (a man) was the Sultan of Swat. Babe Didrikson was the Texas Tornado and Whatta-Gal. Sportswriter Paul Gallico first labeled Didrikson a "muscle moll" in an article he wrote for *Vanity Fair* in 1932. He'd spent an afternoon hitting golf balls with her and discovered she was a pretty good golfer too. He wrote:

"I went through the whole list of sports with her, trying to find something she couldn't do—fencing, bowling, skating, billiards,

Babe Didrikson won thirteen consecutive golf tournaments as an amateur and then became one of the best Ladies Professional Golf Association players of all time. She won thirty-one tournaments, three of them U.S. Opens.

> *"**U**nquestionably the greatest all-around athlete this country has ever produced. There never has been a man who could do half the things she can in sports, or do them as competently."*
>
> —Paul Gallico, 1932

swimming, diving—she is as adept at all of them. Finally I said, 'Great guns, Babe, isn't there anything you don't play?'

'Sure,' she said—'Dolls.'"

Paul Gallico's physical description of Didrikson was probably accurate: about 5 feet 7 inches (170 cm) tall, about 126 pounds (57 kg), and greenish blue eyes. But he added, she had "the biceps of a village blacksmith" and "a light fuzz on her upper lip, her face and her neck." Her hair, he said, was "a mop . . . close-cropped like a boy's." In Paul Gallico's eyes, Didrikson was more masculine than feminine. Others in the media made similar statements. This criticism of her gender identity might have stung her, for she began trying to appear a bit more ladylike. She occasionally wore dresses. And she made a point to tell the press that she liked to sew and cook.

Babe Didrikson, in Paul Gallico's opinion, was "unquestionably the greatest all-around athlete this country has ever produced." He didn't say the best female athlete, either. "There never has been a man who could do half the things she can in sports, or do them as competently," he wrote.

He worried, though, that she wasn't happy. She didn't wear makeup. She didn't date. She called other girls who weren't athletic "sissies." Paul Gallico need not have worried, though. Didrikson was happiest when she was competing. And she was always competing.

In 1935 Babe decided to become a professional golfer. In an interview with *Time* magazine, she said, "Good golf is not a male monopoly. My own case proves it." Although she had only been playing the game for two years, she consistently shot in the seventies and could drive a golf ball farther than most men.

Paul Gallico might not have liked sweaty girl athletes, but Didrikson was different. As a sports fan, he could not help admiring her. "I like her," he concluded. "She's a champion."

CHAPTER FOUR

BYLINES AND HEADLINES

WOMEN WHO WRITE NEWS, WOMEN WHO MAKE NEWS

"*Please know that I am aware of the hazards. I want to do it because I want to do it. Women must try to do things as men have tried. When they fail, their failure must be a challenge to others.*"

—Amelia Earhart, in a letter to her husband (Last Flight, 1937)

Amelia Earhart's last flight (1937) was an attempt to fly solo around the world. When her airplane disappeared over the South Pacific, newspaper headlines (right) reported on the search-and-rescue efforts, providing hope that she might have survived. Her body and the wreckage of her plane were never found.

THE MARCH 1933 ISSUE of *Ladies' Home Journal* was on the newsstands. The magazine featured an interview with the United States' new First Lady, Eleanor Roosevelt. "I do not plan to give up my interests," Roosevelt had told journalist Isabel Leighton. Roosevelt planned to continue to write her news columns and articles and to edit a book called *Babies, Just Babies*. She promised to donate her salary and fees to charities.

The statement was shocking. Roosevelt was breaking tradition. As the magazine writer pointed out, no other First Lady had maintained a career while serving her husband in the White House. "Tradition," the First Lady responded, "unless it is valuable should not count at all. It should be wiped out when it is handicapping and bad."

The First Lady made another startling announcement that also broke tradition: She would hold her own press conferences each Monday morning in the White House. And that wasn't all. Only women reporters could attend. Again, her announcement came with

In April 1934, Eleanor Roosevelt sits at the typewriter in New York City's Newspaper Women's Club. The following year, she would launch a six-day-a-week column as a forum for expressing her views on social and political issues. Titled My Day, the syndicated column ran for twenty-seven years.

a promise. She would not discuss political matters at her press conferences. That was the president's business. Rather, she would focus on social and educational issues.

What was the First Lady thinking? If no other president's wife had held press conferences, why should she? The person who gave her the idea was her close friend Lorena Hickok, who was herself a reporter. Women had a difficult time getting serious news assignments, she explained. They competed against male reporters for the opportunity to cover stories other than social balls and charity fund-raisers. They earned less money than the male reporters. Although women had been in the journalism business since the mid-1800s, they still could not join professional news organizations such as the National Press Club.

President Roosevelt also endorsed the First Lady's press conference idea. His concern was not with the rights of women, however. Rather, he believed the press meetings would be good publicity and help him to gain the support of the American people in passing social welfare programs. Not everyone agreed with the president on this point. Mrs. Roosevelt might make statements that could embarrass or weaken the president's power.

The First Lady may have agreed to the plan for another reason. She could not be someone she wasn't. She had always been outspoken and independent. She needed to do something in the White House other than serving tea. If her press conferences could bring attention to social injustices and inform women of how the political process worked, then that was worthwhile.

On the morning of March 6, 1933, approximately thirty-five newspaper women gathered in the Red Room on the first floor of the White House. Most of these women were strangers to the First Lady. As she stepped inside the room, Roosevelt said she was "trembling." To cover her nervousness, she began the conference by passing around a large box of candy for each reporter to sample.

"Your job is an important one," she told them once the actual meeting began.

> *"Your job is an important one, the idea largely is to make an understanding between the White House and the general public. You [female journalists] are the interpreters to the women of the country."*
> —*Eleanor Roosevelt, 1933*

FIRED, THEN HIRED: RUTH COWAN'S STORY

"I WAS HELL-BENT I was going to make something out of myself," said Ruth Cowan (below). "I didn't know exactly what, but I knew it would be something in the writing field."

She taught school for a few years and then began writing movie reviews for the *San Antonio Evening News*. By the late 1920s, she had an opportunity to write for the United Press (UP) wire service in Austin, Texas. Cowan cleverly concealed that she was a woman by signing her stories R. Baldwin Cowan. Baldwin was her mother's maiden name.

One day, the UP executive editors discovered her game. One of them telephoned the Austin office and asked to speak with Baldwin Cowan.

"You're speaking to her," Ruth answered.

"No, no," he said. "I want to talk to him."

"There ain't no him here," Ruth answered.

A few hours later, the gentleman walked into the office to see for himself just who R. Baldwin Cowan was. He was indeed a she. The man apologized, then fired her. "United Press does not hire women," he said.

Being fired did not stop Ruth Cowan from following her ambition to "make something out of myself." She could continue writing movie reviews or become a society reporter of women's news. But Cowan had greater ambitions. She applied to another national wire service, the Associated Press (AP). This time, she was up front about her identity. "I have just been fired from the United Press because I'm a woman. Haven't you got in your big, extensive organization a place for a woman?"

The AP hired her to work in its Chicago office. She took the train from Texas to Illinois. "They gave me a desk and a typewriter and told me to get busy," she said. Some of her assignments were about women. In the 1930s, she was covering trials in Chicago when Al Capone was arrested. She was at the courthouse one day when she spied the infamous gangster walking toward her. "He was limping," she said. "I looked down, and I said, 'Ooh, new shoes. They hurt, don't they?' And he said 'Yes.'"

That tiny detail, which Cowan included in her story, revealed a personal side to the Chicago gangster. Cowan wove the detail into her lead paragraph. As a result, her story landed on the front page. Ruth Cowan knew then that she was on her way at last to becoming "a first-class reporter."

"The idea largely is to make an understanding between the White House and the general public. You are the interpreters to the women of the country," she said.

The press had long referred to the president as FDR. They began to refer to the First Lady as Mrs. R., or simply ER. ER's press conferences sent news organizations into a tailspin. Most newspapers, magazines, and wire services did not have women reporters on their staffs. Those who did had assigned them to researching and writing stories for the woman's pages. Just as Lorena Hickok had predicted, newspapers now scrambled to hire women writers to cover ER's conferences.

Suddenly, new doors of opportunity for women journalists began to open, if only a little. That little opening was all some women needed to step inside and start their careers as serious news correspondents.

Male editors and publishers did not think that their female reporters were capable of writing hard news. And speaking more to the attitude of the times, they did not consider their female readers capable of reading it.

THE WOMAN'S ANGLE

The 1930s' world of journalism was primarily the province of men. Women could enter but usually through just two specially marked doors: the sob sister story or the woman's page. The sob sisters wrote stories about sensational topics: murders, kidnappings, and social problems such as homeless women, hungry children, and runaway youths. Sob sister reporting could be dangerous. The sisters were daring news hounds who often went undercover, pretending to be someone they weren't in order to sniff out their stories. When writing, the sisters exaggerated details of description in order to strum the heartstrings of their readers and move them to tears. In short, sob sister stories were the soap operas of journalism. In the hard times of the Depression, sensationalism and not always hard-boiled, researched facts sold newspapers.

Mildred Gilman was a sob sister during the 1920s. While covering a murder, she had posed as a nurse to gain access to information about the murder victim's wife. She did it, she said, to get the scoop on other news reporters. She also "slanted stories" to increase the sensationalism. "Embroidered facts were sometimes necessary to titillate the readers," she said. As a sob sister, it was part of the job.

The woman's page writer, on the other hand, focused on the type of stories that newspaper publishers and editors (usually but not always men) assumed women enjoyed reading: fashion trends, social gossip, advice columns on relationships, and community projects such as playgrounds and schools. These were stories that had "a woman's angle." An angle is a story's emphasis. It determines not only which details a reporter includes in a story but also how the story is told. "Put yourself in the place of another," instructed Ethel Brazelton, who taught women students at the Medill School of Journalism at Northwestern University in Chicago. By developing sympathy and understanding, a woman could give her story "personality." Tucked inside the newspaper and often printed just once a week, the woman's page was considered "soft news." Since society assumed women were softer

Journalist Ishbel Ross earned the respect of her male colleagues.

creatures than men—that is, by nature more in tune with their emotions—they were given these assignments.

Hard news was the stuff of front pages. Hard news was urgent, serious. Hard news writing required someone who could gather facts quickly and accurately, then organize them into a logical, compelling story. Women couldn't handle the job, said Stanley Walker, an editor with the *New York Herald Tribune*. They lacked logic. They were sloppy note takers who often got their sources wrong. They wrote emotionally with their hearts and not objectively with their minds.

Ishbel Ross proved Stanley Walker wrong. She worked for him on the *New York Herald Tribune*. He admired her "clear and forthright mind." When on assignment, she had stamina and calm that allowed her to observe closely so that her stories—hard news stories—were vivid with details. The highest compliment a serious newswoman can receive, said Ross, was that she "wrote like a man." Stanley Walker thought she did.

Lorena Hickok, too, was an exception. She didn't care much for sob stories or the

Journalist Lorena Hickok (at right, with scarf) *often traveled with First Lady Eleanor Roosevelt* (left) *to learn more about social problems in the United States.*

woman's angle. Soft news reporting just wasn't challenging enough. In a letter she wrote to a fellow newspaperwoman, Hickok explained, "If you're built as I am mentally, temperamentally, nervously, or however you want to put it . . . you don't get any kick out of it except the thrill that comes out of working on news—real, honest-to-gawd stories." Lorena Hickok was the first woman to work for a wire service, a type of news organization that gathered stories and sent them by telegraph wire to member newspapers around the country. Like Ross, she became a "front-page girl" and one of the few newspaperwomen in the 1920s and early 1930s who earned a byline. A byline is the glory of having your name printed as the author of a story. Not even all male reporters got bylines.

During the 1932 presidential election, Lorena Hickok became an intimate friend of Eleanor Roosevelt. That friendship threatened her objectivity when reporting on the president and the First Lady. Lorena Hickok gave up her position with the Associated Press wire service and instead took a position with the government as a field investigator. She worked for one of the president's closest advisers, Harry Hopkins. Hickok's new assignment: travel the country, go into the homes and factories of poor people, document honestly what you observe, and send back reports for the president's review.

This was not "honest-to-gawd-news." And it didn't deliver the thrills of front-page headlines and bylines. Still, Hickok would need all the skills of a sharp hard news reporter to complete the assignment. She was not the only investigator Harry Hopkins hired, not even the only female investigator. But she would prove to be one of the best.

The Men behind the Women's Magazines

While more women were finding work in the newsrooms of newspapers and magazines, only a few climbed to the top of the career ladder to become managing editors or, better yet, publishers. Cissy Paterson was the first woman publisher of a major newspaper, the *Washington Times-Herald* in Washington, D.C. Paterson had some help in climbing the ladder to its top rung. Her grandfather was Joseph Medill, who was not only the owner of the *Chicago Tribune* but also that city's mayor. Her brother had founded the *New York Daily News*. Only as a result of Paterson's persistent hounding did he agree to give her a job there as a news writer. By 1939 Paterson—who enjoyed her family's wealth even during the Great Depression—succeeded in buying both the *Washington Times-Herald* and the *Washington Tribune* and merging them into one successful publication.

The cover images chosen by editors of ladies' magazines continued to emphasize home and glamour even as women's interests expanded. The 1933 cover at left shows a lovely, impeccably made-up woman. By 1939 the cover choice is still lovely and impeccably made-up—but the fact that she's at the controls of an airplane indicates progress.

BRENDA STARR

BRENDA STARR burst into the comic-book newsroom of *The Flash* in June 1940. She had fiery red hair and eyes that sparkled with stars. She wasn't a sob sister. She was a serious front-page news girl with an added twist— adventure twined around romance. Brenda's daring and curiosity got her into some tough situations, but she always triumphed with her glamorous good looks unscathed.

Brenda Starr was the creation of Dalia Messick. As a little girl with bad eyesight, drawing had been a wonderful escape. Her first job as an artist was drawing greeting cards for a business in Chicago. She later moved to New York City, where she earned the fabulous sum of fifty dollars a week, most of which she sent home to her family.

Throughout the 1930s, the comic-book craze was sweeping the country. Comic books were cheap entertainment. Newspapers, too, began running new comic strips. However, like most jobs in the newspaper world, cartoon artists were usually men.

After editors had rejected her work a number of times, Messick adopted the same trickery as Ruth Cowan had (as had lots of women in the 1930s and 1940s who wanted to break into the traditionally male work world): She changed her first name to Dale. "If I sent in my stuff and they knew I was a woman, they wouldn't even look at it," she said.

The publisher of the *Chicago Tribune* was Joseph Medill. It took a great deal of persuasion, mainly by one of his female staff members, but he reluctantly agreed to publish the comic in all his newspapers except for his prized publication, the *Chicago Tribune*. He refused to have a female cartoonist ink the pages of his favorite paper. Indeed, the first time Brenda appeared in the *Tribune* was after Joseph Medill's death.

Brenda's career has lasted decades. And while many young women who aspired to become journalists might not have known the names of Ishbel Ross or Lorena Hickok, they knew the name of Brenda Starr.

Women's magazines soared in popularity in the 1940s. Many of the old-timers that had been around for decades, such as *Ladies' Home Journal* and *McCall's Magazine*, had changed with the times. Gone were the long and often boring short stories. Gone, too, was the old attitude that women were interested only in homemaking. *Ladies' Home Journal* was publishing articles on alcoholism and essays on Russia.

But some things stayed the same, such as the belief that women lacked the business sense and discipline to run a big-time publication. Otis L. Wiese, the editor of *McCall's*, put it this way: "A woman has the courage to think for herself but not for other women," he said. "It takes a man to do that."

The man behind the *Ladies' Home Journal* was Bruce Gould. He shared the number one position with his wife, Beatrice. This husband-and-wife team, however, divided the tasks of running the magazine: He managed the business end, the corporate affairs. She managed the creative ideas that focused on homemaking and fashions.

Still, just as Cissy Paterson had carved a place in publishing history for women by managing two important newspapers in the nation's capital, some women had earned for themselves the title (and tasks) of editor in chief. Gertrude Lane started with *Woman's Home Companion* as an office girl and even-tually became vice president of the company that owned that magazine. Her secret to her success, she said, was this: "I was a hog for work and so I got ahead."

Even when a woman succeeded in reaching the top management positions, she didn't get credit for being an intelligent, business-savvy woman in her own right. More often than not, her colleagues praised her for thinking "like a man." When Gertrude Lane died, the chairman of her board called her "the best man in the business."

DOCUMENTING THE DUST BOWL

Not all women journalists communicated with pen and paper or even an ink typewriter ribbon. Photographers also documented the news as well as feature stories.

What's the difference between a news story and a feature news story? Timing, in part. For example, the day the stock market crashed on October 29, 1929, was a news event. Reporters rushed to discover the who-what-where-when-and-why of the event. The Great Depression that followed the stock market crash was no news. For one thing, it had gone on too long—years already. News is new, fresh, an unusual event that happens in the "now."

News reporting also includes feature stories. Features provide more in-depth detail about ongoing consequences of a news event.

MIGRANT MOTHERS

POPULAR PHOTOGRAPHY of the 1930s was personal. People paid to have their portraits taken in a photographer's studio. These images did not appear in newspapers or magazines. Rather, they were private memories of someone's life and relationships. Families framed their photographs, hung them on the wall, or set them on a tabletop.

Documentary photography, on the other hand, recorded a social or political situation. These images communicated information and not just memories. Even a single picture could suggest conflict and struggle. The goal of documentary photography, said photographer Roy Stryker, was "to tell not only what a person or a place or a thing looks like but it must also tell the audience what it would feel like to be an actual witness to the scene."

Dorothea Lange's photograph of a migrant mother and her children both shocked and saddened those who saw it.

Roy Stryker worked for the U.S. government in the 1930s as part of President Roosevelt's New Deal programs to help the United States recover from the Depression. FDR hired a team of photographers, many of them women, such as Dorothea Lange, to travel throughout the country, documenting poverty and homelessness. Many of the photographs taken during this period were of women. But these women were not the society debutantes printed on the glossy pages of fashion magazines. Nor were they the carefully created illustrations of middle-class housewives seen in advertisements.

The woman (*above*) was only thirty-two years old, though she looked much older.

Lange sits atop her automobile while traveling through the California countryside, documenting poverty during the Great Depression.

She had lost her home, and she and her children were living in a lean-to tent in a pea-picker's field in California. Lange's camera captured the woman's desperation. Her children were hungry. How would she feed them? "She seemed to know that my pictures might help her," Lange said.

Although Lange's photographs were intended to inform the president and his advisers of the real hardships many Americans were experiencing, the images also appeared in the *San Francisco News* in March 1936. The *Midweek Pictorial* also published the image of the migrant woman and her children with the headline, "Look into her eyes!"

Lange called her photograph "Migrant Mother." The woman in the pea-picker's field became a symbol of the thousands of other suffering migrant mothers. Dorothea Lange's photography did not bring jobs, food, or clothing to those mothers, but it did increase a nation's awareness of the miseries of the Great Depression.

Images such as this 1936 photograph of a North Dakota family sharing a meal made the tragedy of the Dust Bowl drought real to those living in more hospitable climates.

Newspapers print news and occasional short features. Magazines, however, publish full-length feature stories. The Dust Bowl drought in the American Midwest was such a story.

The drought lasted for most of the 1930s, drying up the land and sending great, black clouds of dry soil rolling across the land, often burying houses to the windowsills and choking livestock. The drought did not happen on a single day, the way the crash of the stock market did. The drought was an ongoing and increasingly desperate situation for hundreds of thousands of American farmers and ranchers.

In 1934 *Fortune* magazine sent its star photographer, Margaret Bourke-White, to the American Midwest to document the dust bowl. She traveled first to Omaha, Nebraska, and later to North and South Dakota, following the same routes Lorena Hickok had as she compiled her field reports for FDR. Bourke-White's work, however, would be published in a magazine rather than sent to the president of the United States. Hundreds of thousands of readers would see her pictures. Somehow, she had to capture not just what the drought looked like. She had to capture what it felt like to be a farmer living on this scorched land.

She hired a pilot to fly her over the farmlands. What she saw left her with "disturbing memories." She had never before seen a land so barren, so beaten by the sun, she said. The sun itself was gloomy, hidden behind "curtains of fine-blown soil." The land was "ghostly . . . half-buried" with mounds of soil. She saw "endless dun-colored acres, which should have been green with crops, carved into dry ripples by the aimless winds."

Once the airplane landed, Bourke-White continued her research by meeting with the people who were attempting to scratch a living into the baked, dry soil. Many had given up. They packed everything they owned onto a truck and headed west to California. "I had never seen people caught helpless like this in total tragedy," Margaret Bourke-White would later write in her autobiography. The people were "numb . . . bewildered."

For a short time, Bourke-White felt overwhelmed. "How could I tell it all in pictures?" she wondered. The Dust Bowl assignment not only haunted her memory. It also inspired her to change the focus of her work. At *Fortune* magazine, she had primarily photographed objects for advertising. She realized she wanted to do something more meaningful. "Suddenly it was the people who counted," she said.

At about this same time, an enterprising publisher, Henry Luce, had an idea for a new type of magazine based not on a reporter's observation but on the photographer's eye. Luce's *Life* magazine would feature glossy images of all aspects of life in United States. He intended to hire four photographers, the best he could find. Margaret Bourke-White was one of the four.

"I had never seen people caught helpless like this in total tragedy." The people were "numb . . . bewildered."

—*Margaret Bourke-White* (below), 1963

WOMEN MAKE NEWS, 1933: *Frances Perkins and Social Security*

Just as Eleanor Roosevelt had broken tradition by holding her own press conferences, President Roosevelt also broke tradition when he appointed a woman to serve as secretary of labor. Franklin Roosevelt's cabinet

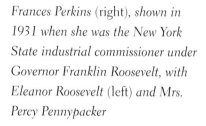

Frances Perkins (right), *shown in 1931 when she was the New York State industrial commissioner under Governor Franklin Roosevelt, with Eleanor Roosevelt* (left) *and Mrs. Percy Pennypacker*

included just ten people, but they were very powerful people. They headed important government departments, such as the Navy and the Treasury. Never in the history of the United States had a woman held a cabinet position. President Roosevelt said he appointed Frances Perkins as secretary of labor because she was smart. She was also a risk taker with liberal ideas about how a country should care for its out-of-work or senior citizens. She had seen the "specter of unemployment" in the United States. Fathers or mothers who could not pay the rent often were evicted from their homes. She saw these bewildered mothers and fathers standing in streets with everything they owned—furniture, pots and pans, bedding—piled in a heap at the curb. They did not know where to go or how to get there.

The United States must do better, Perkins believed. As secretary of labor, she could try to end such social injustices. However, before accepting the president's appointment, she warned him that if appointed, she intended to fight hard for new government policies, including unemployment insurance, old-age insurance, and health insurance. If that's not what you want, then you don't want me, she told him.

"Do you think it can be done?" he asked her.

She answered honestly, "I don't know, but lots of other problems have been solved by the people of the United States, and there is no reason why this one shouldn't be solved."

"Do you think you can do it?" he pressed.

Again, she answered, "I don't know."

And then she added, "But I want to try." The president agreed to let her try. She accepted the cabinet appointment, in part because she believed she could make a change. But she also entered the president's cabinet room in the White House because, she said, the door might not be open again to a woman for a long time.

During her first cabinet meeting, Perkins later recalled she was apprehensive. She purposely held her tongue. She wasn't afraid to speak, she said. She just didn't want to feed the stereotype that women were too talkative. But soon the cabinet and the country would hear from her. She headed a committee to investigate a new government program called Social Security. It would provide income for people who lost their jobs. It would also provide pension to the elderly once they retired. In 1935 Congress passed the Social Security Act. Perkins had succeeded.

WOMEN MAKE NEWS, 1936: *Ruth deForest Lamb and the Rats in the Attic*

Mrs. Roosevelt, *Time* magazine reported, had "started another of her countless crusades, this time against poisonous cosmetics." During one of her Monday morning press conferences, she had shown photographs to the ladies of the press. The photographs showed a woman who had been "horribly blinded" by a cosmetic dye called "Lash Lure." The First Lady had "pressed the pictures to her breast and exclaimed: 'I cannot bear to look at them!'"

The crusade had begun with letters from women across the United States. Some were shocking, such as the letter written by ten-year-old Hazel Fay Brown. Hazel's mother had visited a beauty parlor in a midwestern city where the beautician applied a dye to her eyebrows and lashes. Lash Lure was a type of permanent mascara. It contained a chemical called paraphenylenediamine (PPD). Most women, including the beauticians, had never heard of the chemical. Likewise, most did not know that the chemical could cause severe allergic reactions. Hazel wrote:

> *Dear Mr. President,*
>
> *I am writing this letter for a certain reason, and that is because I don't want anything to happen to other ladies like it has happened to my mother. My mother suffered a great deal by the cause of some poison which was put in the dye and then applied to the lashes. My mother has been trying to put a new law across so that no more poison will be put in this dye. . . . My mother is totally blind and we want you to please help us to get the law across.*

Many of the letters were addressed to the First Lady.

Dear Mrs. Roosevelt,

I have been informed by a number of people that you are interested in this fight against poison cosmetics. . . . I am sure that you are a very busy woman and I will make my story brief as possible and you will have to excuse all mistakes as I am unable to read what I have written.

The woman was thirty years old and lived in Indianapolis, Indiana. She, too, had lost her eyesight. Four years earlier, she explained, she had begun using a cosmetic product called Koremlu Cream. A few days later, she became ill. It was only the beginning of her nightmare.

Koremlu Cream was a cosmetic product developed by a woman named Kora Lublin, who ran a beauty parlor in New York City. Lublin held no medical degree, nor for that matter did she have any knowledge of chemistry. But she knew what women wanted—or rather what they didn't want: hair on their chins, arms, and legs. As someone concerned with women's beauty, she collected formulas for various beauty preparations. She came across an article on thallium acetate. The chemical was ordinarily used as rat poison, but

the news clipping indicated that it removed hair. A French "authority" had added the chemical to an ointment and used it for treating scalp diseases, quite possibly dandruff. The Frenchman, however, had stopped making the ointment because of "many accidents."

Kora Lublin saw an opportunity to make money on a new beauty product. She advertised Koremlu Cream as "'Nature's rival' that creates baldness only where it is applied." The directions advised applying the cream at night, "the same as any good cold cream." The advertisement reassured the public that the cream was safe. According to the advertisement, Koremlu Cream "is unlike anything ever used before and offers for the first time real freedom from superfluous hair."

To create Koremlu, the workers in Kora Lublin's laboratory mixed two 100-gram (3.5-ounce) jars of thallium acetate into a cream base. From this mixture, they bottled 150 jars of the product. But the laboratory workers did not measure how much of the chemical went into each jar. Some jars contained none or only traces of the rat poison. Other jars contained a great deal more. Without regulations, each batch varied.

Kora Lublin's beauty product was a success. Even large department stores sold it. Then the nightmares began. For some women, the cream was harmless. They were the lucky ones who had purchased jars with little or no thallium acetate. Others were not so fortunate. The woman from Indianapolis who wrote to Mrs. Roosevelt suffered for four years. At first, doctors said she needed to have some teeth removed. But her condition became worse. She suffered paralysis of her feet and could not walk. Eventually, her eyesight began to fail. At the Mayo Clinic in Minnesota, doctors identified the cause of her sickness: thallium acetate poisoning. They could do nothing for her. The poison was throughout her body. She lost her job and her means to earn a living. She ended her letter with a plea:

There are laws to punish people for committing murders and it seems as though there could be something to prevent carelessness that wrecks lives and makes people invalids all of their remaining days, which is far worse than death. Mrs. Roosevelt, please don't think I have grown bitter and sour on life because I have not. . . . I just want to help others from having the same thing happen in their lives.

This is the manufacturer's version of the effect of this aniline eyelash dye.

The New and Improved for Brow and Eye Lash Dye
LASH lure
Radiates Personality

Total blindness was its actual effect in at least one instance.

Before

After

"There are laws to punish people for committing murders and it seems as though there could be something to prevent carelessness that wrecks lives and makes people invalids all of their remaining days, which is far worse than death."

—an Indiana woman, in a letter to Eleanor Roosevelt about the toxic effects of Lash Lure (above), 1936

Koremlu Cream and Lash Lure were not the only cosmetic or food products being sold in the 1920s and 1930s that proved to be dangerous, if not deadly. At the time, federal laws did not apply to cosmetics. Often the advertisements for these products and many others made promises that simply weren't truth. Mrs. America wanted to be beautiful, yes. But she did not want to be swindled. Often the manufactured products were not intended to harm anyone. But without proper testing, the public could not be certain that a product was safe. On the other hand, many more products were pure and simple quackery.

Ruth deForest Lamb was the chief education officer in the U.S. Food and Drug Administration (FDA), one of the few women to hold such an important position in a government agency. She supported new laws to protect the consumer from false advertising and dangerous products. Angry protests came from the cosmetic industry as well as the advertisers. Most feared they would lose most of their business if their advertising had to remove any exaggerated claims. "The opponent ... will tell you," she wrote, "if Government officials had their way, you couldn't even take an aspirin tablet with a doctor's prescription. ... Those fanatics in Washington want to burn down the house to get rid of a few rats in the attic."

Ruth deForest Lamb

The "fanatics" were not just Ruth deForest Lamb, the president, and the First Lady. They also included hundreds of women from organizations across the country such as the General Federation of Women's Clubs, The American Home Economics Association, and the Medical Women's National Association. The "rats in the attic" were the few businesses that made unsafe products. The only problem was, there weren't just two rats—Lash Lure and

Koremlu. There weren't even just a few. There were hundreds, as FDA research later proved.

In 1936 Ruth deForest Lamb helped to prepare an FDA exhibit called the Chamber of Horrors. She wrote a book that year with the same title, detailing the stories of men and women who had suffered and sometimes died from unsafe products. Both the exhibit and the book provided photographs to illustrate the horrors as well as the untruthful advertising used to promote the products. Also included were letters written by the victims.

Two years later, a new federal drug law went into effect. Not everyone was happy with the law. Compromises were made, the FDA admitted. All the same, under the new law, drug manufacturers were required to provide scientific proof that new products could be safely used before putting them on the market. And for the first time ever, cosmetics were included in that regulation. Elizabeth Arden bristled when she had to change the label on her favorite best-selling product, Orange Skin Food. The cream was not a nutrient, the FDA ruled. The name was misleading the public. Elizabeth Arden presented her own batch of letters from satisfied

Using materials originally assembled for U.S. Senate hearings on the legislation that became the Federal Food, Drug, and Cosmetic Act of 1938, the U.S. Food and Drug Administration created a traveling exhibit called the Chamber of Horrors. The intent was to show consumers how to read labels and determine the quality of a product.

customers, including one who said her cook had thought the cream (which the woman kept in the refrigerator) was icing and mistakenly applied it to a cake that everyone ate. No one became ill.

In the years and decades to come, medical quackery and advertising exaggerations would continue to test the limits of the law. For now, however, Mrs. America had won the first battle.

Women Make News, 1937: *Amelia Earhart's Final Flight*

In 1932 Amelia Earhart had become the first woman to pilot an airplane solo across the Atlantic Ocean. "I want to do it because I want to do it," she told her husband.

Throughout the 1920s, Amelia Earhart had made headlines for her flying adventures and endurance records. After only ten hours of flight instruction in 1920, she made her first solo flight. She set speed, altitude, and endurance records for flight. Her list of firsts was impressive: the first woman to fly from Hawaii in the South Pacific Ocean to Oakland, California; the first woman to fly nonstop across the United States; and the first woman to receive the Distinguished Flying Cross. She sat on aeronautical boards and was the aviation editor for *Cosmopolitan* magazine. She said she did it all "for the fun of it."

But there was another reason for daring

exploits. "Women must try to do things as men have tried. When they fail, their failure must be a challenge to others." Amelia Earhart was one of the best-known women in America and one of the most daring.

In 1937 she attempted to set a new record by flying around the world. On July 2, however, somewhere near Howland Island in the Pacific Ocean, all communications from her ended. The world waited to hear of her fate. Navy ships and airplanes searched for some sign of wreckage and found noth-ing. She might have crashed into the ocean or perhaps she had somehow managed to land on an uncharted island. After two weeks, however, the U.S. government had little hope of finding her alive.

Rumors swirled. Her world flight was more than a publicity stunt. It was a cover-up for a secret government assignment. Amelia Earhart was spying on the Japanese for the U.S. Navy. Japanese aggression in the South Pacific had been growing throughout the decade. Some said the Japanese had shot

Was she an adventurous aviatrix or a U.S. spy? Some people believed that Amelia Earhart's disappearance in 1937 wasn't an accident and that she was shot down while spying on the Japanese military in the South Pacific.

down her airplane. Others believed the Japanese had taken her prisoner.

No proof surfaced of the government having sent Amelia Earhart on a secret mission. The rumors persisted, perhaps because Americans did not want to believe that someone so capable, so courageous could fail.

WOMEN MAKE NEWS, 1938: *Pearl S. Buck's Prize*

On an autumn morning in 1938, the telephone rang in Pearl S. Buck's apartment in New York City. Buck was sitting at her desk in her study, writing. Her adopted children were playing outside on the terrace with their nurse. She picked up the telephone and heard her secretary exclaim excitedly, "You've been awarded the Nobel Prize!"

"Wo *pu hsiang hsin*," said the writer. In her surprise, she had responded in Chinese, a language she knew fluently. The phrase meant: "I don't believe it."

A second telephone in the apartment rang. This time her husband brought her the same incredible news: the Nobel Committee at the Swedish Academy in Sweden had selected Pearl S. Buck to receive their prize in literature for 1938.

Even then Buck insisted it must be the rumor of an aggressive reporter. Pearl Buck was well known. Her novel about China, *The Good Earth*, had been a best-seller for many years and just a year earlier had been made into an equally popular Hollywood film. Only after her husband telephoned Sweden himself and confirmed the news did the author believe the honor to be real. She was the first American woman ever to receive the Nobel Prize in Literature. In fact, she was only the third American writer to be so honored.

The Nobel Prize is the highest honor a writer from any nation might ever hope to achieve. And yet, Buck had an uneasy feeling about it—and she was right. Upon hearing the news that Pearl Buck had won the award, poet Robert Frost commented sourly, "If she can get it, anybody can!" Many other American writers, mostly men, also criticized the committee's choice. They wrote articles against Buck that appeared in magazines such as the *Saturday Evening Post*. Pearl Buck's novels were popular among everyday people, especially women. They were, her critics cried, "too popular" and too simple to be taken as serious literature. Furthermore, she wrote about China, which in the eyes of many Americans was at the time a backward, uncivilized country of peasants. Some Asians argued that an American woman could not possibly understand and write from the point of view of the Chinese, even if she had lived among them for many years. If the Nobel Committee wanted to honor someone for writing about China, it should be a Chinese author. Still others objected to her receiving the Nobel Prize for no other reason than that she was a woman.

These criticisms from her fellow writers stung. They were "a sort of stone-throwing," she said, and the stones filled her with self-doubt. Perhaps she was not worthy to accept the Nobel Prize. She was miserable and melancholy. Then one night at dinner, she met Sinclair Lewis for the first time. This American writer had won the Nobel Prize in Literature a few years earlier. "Don't let anyone minimize for you the receiving of the Nobel Prize," he told her. "It is a tremendous event. Enjoy every minute of it for it will be your finest memory."

He spoke to her at length as if he understood every doubt she had been feeling. "Never mind people," he told her. "Never mind!"

And so, Pearl Buck packed her suitcase for the journey to Sweden. She kissed her young children good-bye. Leaving them behind was the most difficult part of her journey. She, her husband, and their eldest daughter boarded a ship bound for Europe. What she would discover there would cause her to feel great dread.

Accepting the Nobel Prize from King Gustav of Sweden filled her with joy, just as Sinclair Lewis had promised it would. And yet, beyond the grand banquet hall and the rooms of the Swedish Academy, not all was right. "Anxiety was stifling in the air," she said. In China she had lived through revolutions and war. Now, she could see that war was threatening Europe. She could almost smell the malice in the air. The Great War, which would later become known as World War I (1914–1918), had ended with Germany defeated, and the German Kaiser was long dead. "Someone much worse than the old Kaiser was now in Germany," she wrote, "someone more evil."

Pearl Buck, the first American woman to receive the Nobel Prize in Literature, is shown here accepting the prize from King Gustavus V in Stockholm in December 1938.

That someone was Adolf Hitler.

Although she had lived her childhood and young adult life in China, Pearl S. Buck was truly a new American woman. She knew her mind and she spoke it. In America, she refused to live in any southern state that had laws discriminating against black people. "I could not live . . . ," she said, "where I would have always to look at signs to see where I belonged in railroad stations and restaurants."

And so it was not surprising that, while in Europe to receive her Nobel Prize, she refused an invitation to visit Germany where Hitler's policies discriminated against Jews, Roma (Gypsies), and other groups. Her refusal made headlines. "Wouldn't you like to visit Germany?" a reporter from Denmark asked her.

The newspaper quoted her blunt response: "I do not wish to visit a country where I am not allowed to think and speak freely. . . . I am an individualist and a Democrat."

"I do not wish to visit a country [Germany] where I am not allowed to think and speak freely. . . . I am an individualist and a Democrat."

—Pearl S. Buck, 1938

Perhaps it was on the journey home across the Atlantic Ocean that Pearl Buck came to an understanding about herself and her life. The Nobel Prize was both an honor and a challenge. Far more important to her than being a remarkable writer, she said, was being a remarkable woman.

WOMEN MAKE NEWS, 1939: *Marian Anderson's Concert*

Early in 1939, opera star Marian Anderson hoped to present a concert in Constitution Hall in the nation's capital. The owner of the building was an organization called the Daughters of the American Revolution (DAR). To belong to this patriotic group, a woman eighteen years or older had to prove that her family's ancestors had participated in America's fight for independence from Great Britain during the 1700s. This socially prominent group refused to allow Marian Anderson to perform in their hall. All dates were taken, they said.

All dates? The message was quite clear. The problem was not scheduling a free evening. Nor was it Miss Anderson's musical ability. Throughout the 1930s, the concert halls of Europe had welcomed her enthusiastically. "A voice like yours is heard only once in 100 years," the great orchestra conductor Arturo Toscanini reportedly told her.

The problem was Miss Anderson herself. She was African American.

The news angered many people, including America's First Lady. Eleanor Roosevelt was a lifetime member of the DAR. In a letter she wrote to the president of the organization, she resigned from membership:

> *"I am in complete disagreement with the attitude taken in refusing Constitution Hall to a great artist. You have set an example which seems to me unfortunate, and I feel obliged to send in to you my resignation. You had an opportunity to lead in an enlightened way and it seems to me that your organization has failed."*
>
> —*February 26, 1939, National Archives and Records Administration*

The president of the DAR, Mrs. Henry M. Robert Jr., responded, writing on the stationery of the Daughters of the American Revolution: "Our society is engaged in the education for citizenship and the humanitarian service in which we know you to be vitally interested. I am indeed sorry not to have been in Washington at this time. Perhaps I might have been able to remove some of the misunderstanding and to have presented to you the attitude of the society."

What was the "attitude" that Mrs. Robert wished to explain (but did not) in her letter? A few years earlier, the DAR had adopted a policy that "white artists only" could perform in Constitution Hall. They had done so as a way of avoiding "mixed" seating of the races within the auditorium.

Eleanor Roosevelt said that her resignation would likely make "little difference" to the DAR. On that point, she was correct. The DAR did not reverse its attitude. However, the First Lady's resignation brought national attention to the controversy and Marian Anderson's accomplishments as a concert singer. "Mrs. Franklin D. Roosevelt [has been] increasingly vocal these days on national issues," *Time* reported. The magazine noted that the First Lady had not only resigned from the DAR but had made a point to attend a number of African American shows in New York City. Audiences, the magazine noted, stood and applauded her as she entered.

Marian Anderson reacted to the DAR's rejection with quiet dignity but not defeat.

Eleanor Roosevelt (above) *invited Marian Anderson* (left) *to sing at the Lincoln Memorial in 1939 after she was turned away by Constitution Hall. The event drew a record-breaking crowd of seventy-five thousand people. The First Lady presented the Spingarn Medal to Anderson in July 1939* (above), *acknowledging the singer's contribution to the struggle for racial equality.*

"There are people who will, if they want something . . . fight," she said. "And those people are very, very necessary." She, however, was not one of them. Instead, she hoped she could make a difference by doing something worthwhile. For her, that was singing.

Although Marian Anderson was not a fighter, thousands of "irate Washingtonians" rallied in her favor. First Lady Eleanor Roosevelt, the U.S. Department of the Interior, as well as the National Association for the Advancement of Colored People (NAACP) joined hands to organize an outdoor concert featuring Marian Anderson. For the stage, they selected the Lincoln Memorial. On April 9, Easter Sunday after-noon, Marian Anderson stepped from a small room that is behind the very large sculpture of Abraham Lincoln. She stood before a bank of microphones that would carry her voice out to the seventy-five thousand people—both black and white—who had come to hear her sing. The radio microphones, too, would carry her concert into homes across the country. Her first song was "America (My Country, 'Tis of Thee)."

Not until 1942 did the Daughters of the American Revolution make amends to Marian Anderson. They invited her to sing in Constitution Hall. Anderson was a humble person, her nephew remembered. She did not hold grudges. She accepted their invitation.

Chapter Five

The Many Faces of Rosie

The women worked in pairs. I was the riveter and this big, strong, white girl from a cotton farm in Arkansas worked as the bucker. The riveter used a gun to shoot rivets through the metal and fasten it together. The bucker used a bucking bar on the other side of the metal to smooth out the rivets. Bucking was harder than shooting rivets; it required more muscle. Riveting required more skill.

—Sybil Lewis, riveter for Lockheed aircraft, Los Angeles, during World War II

Norman Rockwell

On the eve of World War II,

most Americans held a common belief that men and women possessed unequal physical and mental abilities. Masculine abilities included whacking a golf ball 250 yards (230 m); writing a hard news story fast and accurately; and playing the trumpet, saxophone, and drums. Feminine abilities were looking great in a bathing suit and high heels, writing a sob sister story full of sympathy and emotion, and playing the piano or violin. Men's and women's behaviors seemingly differed too. Men were hard-boiled, competitive, and practical. Women were soft-boiled, nurturing, and romantic. Men understood the value of a dollar. Women were impulsive spenders.

The U.S. government did not create these sweeping generalizations about men and women. However, on the Sunday morning of December 7, 1941, when Japan bombed the U.S. naval base at Pearl Harbor, Hawaii, all assumptions about women had to change . . . if only temporarily. The United States declared war against Japan the next day, officially joining World War II.

In a fireside chat early in 1942, President Roosevelt explained what the United States had to do to win the war against the Axis

Above: *Explosions decimate the planes at Pearl Harbor's Hickham Field during the surprise Japanese attack on the U.S. Navy base, December 7, 1941.* Facing page: Rosie to the Rescue *by Norman Rockwell, 1943*

As World War II began, women viewed their role as being supportive of their men overseas. These women (above) collected pots and pans for a scrap-metal drive in the 1940s. The scrap metal would be melted down and used for manufacturing metal items for the war effort. As the war continued, women were asked to play greater roles, not only on the home front but as nurses in the field.

powers of Germany, Italy, and Japan. First, the country needed soldiers. Already men were enlisting in all branches of the military. Millions more would be drafted into service. Second, the country needed to build weapons, and the statistics were staggering: in the first year, the government would build sixty thousand airplanes, forty-five thousand tanks, and twenty thousand antiaircraft guns.

If men were fighting overseas, who then was going to build the United States' arsenal of war? If men left their jobs in industry, transportation, and business, who then was going to take their places? Who was going to run the country's trains and buses, farm the land, and cut its forests? To win this war, the United States needed women as well as men.

But first, the government had to convince the factory and business owners that women could do whatever job was necessary—from building planes and ships to working on the nation's railroads. Equally important, the government had to persuade American women (and their husbands and fathers) that women *should* work for the good of their country. Millions of working-class women already held jobs. They needed little convincing to take a new position for higher wages in a factory building airplanes, ships, or ammunition. But the government needed millions more.

Convincing white middle-class housewives who probably didn't need extra money and had never worked outside their homes to take a job would not be easy.

The OWI's 3 Rs

Propaganda is the spreading of ideas or beliefs toward a specific goal or policy. It can be either good or bad, depending on the message and its purpose. During World War II, the U.S. government's Office of War Information (OWI) propaganda campaign focused on three key points: rationing, recycling, and recruitment.

Rationing was controlling the consumption of certain products. Gasoline, for example, was needed for war vehicles, so Americans were allowed only so much gas per month for their private cars. Likewise, food products became scarce. Government ration stamps allowed families to purchase coffee, meat, and sugar in carefully controlled portions.

Recycling was saving and reusing valuable materials such as nylon, rubber, tin, and aluminum. Even grease from cooking could be salvaged and reused.

Recruitment was the hiring or enlistment of people as soldiers in the military or as workers in the nation's war industries. The government's efforts to rally Americans to support these three Rs had a noble purpose: the defense of the county's freedoms and the defeat of its enemies.

While all U.S. citizens were included in the OWI propaganda campaign, women, in particular, were the targets of many of these posts. Women, not men, were largely responsible for managing the home, and that included shopping for food, preparing meals, and recycling whatever the family had used. The OWI's three Rs, therefore, appeared in places women frequented, including beauty parlors and grocery stores.

The U.S. Office of War Information worked to get people on the home front involved in the war effort. These posters represent the OWI's three Rs (from top): Rationing, Recycling, and Recruitment.

The OWI posters portrayed working women as feminine, no matter what their assigned job. The welder (left) seems to have some ruffles over her white, puffed sleeves. And the exquisitely coiffed she-soldier from the Women's Army Corps (WAC) (right) is wearing makeup fit for a Hollywood star.

War industry jobs were often demanding and physically exhausting—operating heavy machinery or welding metals. National polls had shown that most middle-class husbands did not want their wives to work, especially in dangerous and dirty factories. Most wives agreed. Also, the average housewife didn't know an acetylene torch from a flashlight. The persuaders had to convince these women that they not only *should* do the job but also *could* do the job.

The government had to make one persuasive point. Once the war was won, the women would happily give up their jobs and return to their homes.

An act of Congress had given the U.S. government the right to draft men into the military. But the government had no legal power to force women to take jobs outside the homes. What was needed was a national propaganda campaign.

The Persuaders

Weeks after the declaration of war, President Roosevelt created the Office of War Information to plan and control the release of information to the public about the war. One of the OWI's propaganda campaigns was the recruitment of womanpower. The

The OWI recruitment posters appealed to women by stressing the pride and gratitude they would receive from others—especially the men in their lives.

government needed two types of women workers: military recruits, or "she-soldiers," and civilian recruits to work both in war industries and also to replace men who had left their peacetime jobs to go to war.

To recruit she-soldiers, the War Department created a woman's branch of the army, called the Women's Army Corps, or WACs for short. She-soldiers could not shoot a gun, but they could do clerical and technical work. The she-soldiers served at home and overseas, freeing men to fight on the front lines. The navy, too, had its woman's branch, called Women Accepted for Volunteer Emergency Service, or WAVES.

The OWI recruited she-soldiers by appealing to women's patriotism. OWI posters showed women in crisp, well-tailored military uniforms. The text suggested that women were enlisting to support their loved ones—sweethearts, husbands, or fathers. By enlisting, women could end the war sooner and bring those loved ones home.

Patriotism wasn't enough, however. The OWI had to persuade the country that women in military service were still feminine, not masculine. And so each woman depicted on the military recruitment posters was very pretty, even glamorous. She had healthy, glowing skin. She wore lipstick and mascara. Her hair was neatly pinned beneath her military cap. African American women also enlisted in armed services. However, the OWI poster images were of white women.

"It took more than a well-tailored uniform to change an American girl into an American service woman," said news reporter Walter Cronkite. "It took perseverance, courage, hard work and a willingness to learn new disciplines and new skills." Language like that also appealed to a woman's pride and self-esteem. The OWI military recruitment campaign worked. Hundreds of thousands of American women enlisted, and their service would prove essential to winning the war.

To recruit the civilian workers, OWI used the same emotional appeals: patriotism, glamour, and pride. They also added one more—fear. As the campaign began, hundreds of posters began appearing in cities and small towns across the United States, both in public places, such as post offices, and in workplaces. On one poster, a dirty child looks pleadingly at the viewer. Behind her is the sky filled with smoke and a large swastika, the symbol of the German Nazis, the United States' enemy in the war. The headline read: "Deliver us from evil." American women were being asked to ration food and to recycle household by-products. If women failed, then evil—Hitler and the Nazi forces—would overrun the world.

Images of the horrible things that were happening to civilians in the nations where World War II was being fought were used to spur production on the U.S. home front.

Not all poster images were quite so grim. One showed a drawing of a beautiful woman with red lips and piercing, heavy-lashed eyes. Her hair is swept up revealing her neck. She wears a fur around her shoulders. She is meant to be attractive, but the text suggests that her glamour is really a trap. "Allure or a lure?" the text asks. "Always be careful! Don't talk about military affairs." The women in this image is someone a soldier should fear.

The OWI did not work alone, however.

Nor were posters the only method of persuasion. The newly formed War Advertising Council worked with the OWI to create advertisements that would appear in the magazines and newspapers that women read. Songwriters, too, created popular music on the OWI's themes of rationing, recycling, and recruitment. These songs played over and over on the radio and in jukeboxes in diners and dance halls. Other persuaders included fiction writers, entertainers, and Hollywood filmmakers.

American women were encouraged to use their new wartime income to buy War Bonds. The purchase of these bonds helped fund the U.S. war effort.

As a result, the image of American womanhood changed dramatically. Advertisements in the 1930s that had focused on housewives troubled by "domestic hands" now showed women operating heavy factory machinery and declaring they weren't "softies." In the 1930s, Pond's had showcased the youthful complexions of society women in its advertisements for facial creams. During the war, Pond's stressed that its facial creams could keep a factory girl's skin "adorably pretty."

In movie houses, short documentary films played to mostly female audiences, urging them to get a job in wartime factories. *Glamour Girls of 1943* showed women operating factory machines, sewing parachutes, and inspecting machine parts on an assembly line. It also showed women in nonindustrial jobs, as well, such as driving a bus or farming. In the late 1930s, actress Loretta Young played romantic comedy roles. By 1942, however, Loretta Young's movie roles had changed. A newsreel from 1942 showed the popular actress filming a scene for a new movie, *China*. She is playing an American schoolteacher living in China and fighting against the Japanese. In the 1930s, Loretta Young played the unhappy bishop's wife helped by an angel. When the director calls "Cut!" the actress turns to the camera. She is not acting now.

"I want particularly to speak to you women in this theater," she begins. "We've found that the hand that rocks the cradle can build bombs, make ammunition, and turn every kitchen into a salvage station for vitally needed war materials," she says. "Yes, they can even help to finance this war, too."

And yet, the actress added, "None of us—no matter how much we've done—are doing enough." Loretta Young's newsreel message used a fear appeal, warning women that if they didn't get involved, they risked losing what they valued most: their home and children. "There is a job for each and every one of us and it is our duty to find that job. Because every job we do is a pledge that our homes will not be destroyed. And every [government war] bond we buy is a promise that our children will not grow up in bondage."

Even walking down the street, a woman could not escape the OWI messages targeted at her. Images of working women appeared on billboards. Slogans such as "We can do it" and "Use it up, wear it out, make it do, or do without" appeared on the sides of trucks and buses. They were printed too on bread wrappers, diaper bags, and other objects that women were likely to use.

One persuasive strategy was to compare industrial work to housework. "If you followed recipes exactly in making cakes, you can learn to load shells," stated one advertisement. An advertisement for 3-M machines compared riveting to sewing. "Give them a rivet gun for a needle, sheets of aluminum for material, and these workers will stitch you an airplane wing in half the time it used to take."

In 1941 more than thirty million women were housewives. By 1944 approximately six million had left their homes to work, either in military or civilian positions. That is a small percentage—clearly more women stayed at home than went to work. Even so, the OWI campaign promoting the three Rs—rationing, recycling, and especially recruitment of womanpower—was successful. "Rosies" had entered the workplace.

Rosies, Rosies Everywhere

Rosie's first public appearance was on a poster created by the OWI in the months following the attack on Pearl Harbor. It showed a white woman wearing a polka-dot bandana wrapped around her hair and a blue work shirt with the sleeves rolled up. She is flexing her right arm, showing muscle. The text reads, "We can do it!"

We Can Do It!

POST FEB. 15 TO FEB. 28

WAR PRODUCTION CO-ORDINATING COMMITTEE

From the time she was introduced by the OWI in 1942, expectations of Rosie were high. She had children and a house to care for, a victory garden to plant, war bonds to buy, and new skills to learn for her full-time job.

The label Rosie the Riveter wasn't used, not yet. That came a few months later, when the May 29, 1943, issue of the *Saturday Evening Post* hit the newsstands. On the cover was a woman. She wears navy overalls and safety goggles pushed up onto her forehead. A heavy riveting gun lays across her lap, perfectly balanced. She holds a sandwich in one hand. Her gray metal lunch box has her name printed on it in block letters. She is a big woman, not fat but brawny. Her shirtsleeves, too, are rolled up past her elbows, revealing muscled biceps. This was no Hollywood goddess or social debutante. Nor was she a resourceful housewife planting her own Victory Garden vegetables. Rosie's posture—sitting on what looks to be a block of wood with her head cocked to one side and chin lifted—suggests confidence. The red, white, and blue flag behind her links her with the United States. Rosie's patriotic. And even though she's mannish in physique, she still has a touch of glamour. She wears makeup. Her lips and cheeks are rosy red, just like her socks.

"She is the home-front equivalent of G.I. Joe," says Sheridan Harvey, a women's studies specialist with the Library of Congress. GI Joes were combat soldiers. Although Rosie wasn't in combat, she was still fighting in the war. The magazine image shows a copy of Adolf

Hitler's book *Mein Kampf* in which he outlines his plan to rule the world. The illustrator, Norman Rockwell, placed the book under Rosie's feet. "The implication is clear," says Sheridan Harvey, "through her defense job, she will help to crush Hitler."

For weeks after the magazine appeared, people wondered: Who was this woman? Rose Hicker was a riveter at the Eastern Aircraft Company in Tarrytown, New York. Was she the real Rosie? Or was it Rose Will Monroe, who worked at the Ford Motor Company aircraft assembly plant in Michigan?

In fact, Rosie wasn't one woman at all. By 1943 many thousands of women were working in factories producing war materials. Most of these Rosies were not middle-class housewives. They were working-class women who had held jobs prior to the war. And many were women of color. Sybil Lewis, for example, was an African American riveter for Lockheed Aircraft in Los Angeles. "You . . . put on your pants, and took your lunch pail to a man's job. This was the beginning of women's feeling that they could do something more," she said. Kay Lamphear was of American Indian heritage. Ruth Mae Moy Wong was of Chinese heritage. Although they, too, were Rosies, their images were not on the cover of a national magazine. Nor were they featured in war-related advertisements.

Not all Rosies were riveters, either. Many different types of Rosies worked all across the United States: single girls, wives, mothers, and

Norman Rockwell's Rosie gave visual form to the new role of the American woman and the crucial role she was expected to play in defending her country.

Although images of Asian American and African American women did not appear on U.S. propaganda posters or magazine covers, these government photographs clearly document that minority women in the United States were also patriotic Rosies.

widows. Some worked in factories, and others worked in offices. Some wore military uniforms, others wore nursing caps, and still others wore baseball caps. All these images of Rosie, however, share the same two characteristics: they are confident and competent women.

"Victory waits on *your* fingertips," stated one OWI poster. A young girl wearing a white blouse and with a blue and red ribbon pinned in her blonde shoulder-length hair sits behind a typewriter. With her right hand to her forehead, she is saluting as if she were in the military. As Rosie the government girl, this patriotic typist was a soldier on the home front too.

Just as the government had once hired photographers to document the Great Depression, so too did the wartime government hire photographers to document its womanpower campaign. These photographs differed from the idealized images of the OWI posters and the magazine advertisements. They documented real Rosies at work. These Rosies did not always wear makeup or have pretty, clean hair or hands. A good number of the photographs were of women of color. In addition to Rosie the Riveter, the government photographs showed Rosie the stenographer, Rosie the train conductor, Rosie the drugstore clerk, Rosie the laundry worker, Rosie the lumberjack—or rather "lumberjill," as one photographic caption described women who worked in timber mills.

Don't Be a Bad Rosie

In 1943 "Rosie the Riveter" was a popular song in the United States. The lyrics praised the achievements of working women. The opening lines, however, scolded those selfish women who were not yet doing their part.

While other girls attend a favorite cocktail bar,
Sipping dry martinis, munching caviar,
There's a girl who's really putting them to shame,
Rosie is her name.

Shame and guilt were among the strategies of the OWI propaganda campaign for womanpower. Women who didn't take a job or who didn't support the war in other ways, such as recycling or rationing, were unpatriotic. They were the "bad Rosies."

A *Collier's* magazine advertisement from 1943 showed a young woman at work in safety gloves and glasses. Both her husband and her father were in Japanese prison camps. She had four children, but she worked a full shift in the factory. Not only that, each payday she invested 25 percent of her wages to purchase war bonds. "That's American fighting spirit," the advertisement stated. Chester LaRoche, who headed the War Advertising Council, believed that if advertisers used the right strategy in appeal-ing to the public, fewer American men would die in the war.

A 1943 poster entitled "It's Our Fight Too!" portrays a Rosie who is fiercely determined to do her part to win the war.

"The citizen must be convinced that, unless he (or she) cooperates, he personally will pay a penalty, either through loss of the war or through loss of something precious to him—his son in the armed forces, his political rights and social privileges, his future freedom." As a result, many advertisements and OWI images showed women at work with the accompanying text stating that their jobs would bring their loved ones home sooner. The flip side of that logic, however, is that loved ones would not return if women didn't go to work. Those "bad Rosies" put U.S. fighting men at risk.

Even the bad Rosie was a myth. By 1944 only one out every eight housewives had taken a job outside the home. With so many women still at home, it is unlikely that they would have viewed one another with scorn.

The Problem with Working Women

"Women scare me," said Joe the Foreman, "At least they do in a factory." Joe is a character in a U.S. government training film that addressed the problems of supervising a wartime factory full of female workers. If all these new workers were men, Joe said, he'd know how to talk to them, set them straight about how to do the job right. But he wasn't quite sure how to talk to or train women.

The government produced *Supervising Women Workers* in 1944, at the height of war production, to help business and industrial managers deal with the specific problems women workers presented. One problem was that women asked for time off a bit too frequently. They aren't shirking their duties, the film instructed. Rather, they may have responsibilities at home, including the care of children.

A more serious problem was training the female worker. "Women weren't naturally familiar with mechanical principles or machines," the film stated. To make its point about masculine and feminine abilities, the film offered this comparison: Asking Rosie to weld an airplane propeller was just about as crazy as asking Joe the Foreman to bake a pie. He'd be no good at it, at least not at first. The film contained misleading information. Many women weren't familiar with machin-

"*I always add an extra pinch of nitroglycerin.*"

A 1942 cartoon by Gardner Rea pokes a bit of fun at women who suddenly found themselves building bombs rather than baking cakes.

ery but not because they lacked a natural ability to understand how machines work. A more likely reason was that schools had not taught girls the principles of machinery, limiting classes such as machine shop to boys only. The film also made sweeping generalizations, such as these:

- When breaking in a new worker, and of course especially a woman, you've got to explain every angle of the process down to the last detail.
- Women can be awfully jealous of each other.
- Women are more sensitive than men.

The "Jenny on the job" poster series was issued in 1943 as way of offering military wives coping skills for their new roles.

Apparently, those beliefs were the reason why Joe the Foreman found female factory workers "scary." Factory workers weren't the only scary women in the United States during the war. "Paper dolls" was the name given to the Rosies who worked in newsrooms, taking over the front-page assignments that had once gone to male reporters. Walter Lister of the *Philadelphia Record* thought the paper dolls spelled poorly and didn't ask the right news questions. Walter Bodin, city editor of the *Oakland Tribune*, stated, "No matter how able they are, all are given to chattering among themselves."

Government-produced posters and publications as well as magazine advertisements praised women's accomplishments. Of course, those media messages were created with the intention of attracting more women into the workplace, and so they were meant to sound positive. Still, statements such as "Good work sister: We never figured you for a man-sized job!" or "Women workers can be surprisingly good producers" revealed ongoing prejudices about women's abilities. "Women Are Writing the News!" was the headline in the *Christian Science Monitor* in a September 1943 issue. The exclamation point communicated surprise. A Chrysler magazine advertisement stated that automobile parts were being "made by women!" Those three words were in big, bold print. The surprise might have been finding women in places where men previously had worked. Then again, the surprise might also have been that women were, in fact, proving to be capable at their new jobs.

"We never figured you could do a man-size job!"

—U.S. government poster, 1944

Rosie at Bat

President Roosevelt believed that baseball games were a cheap form of entertainment during wartime, a great way for people to relax a little and get their minds off the war. He even encouraged baseball owners to hold night games so more people could attend. However, all professional baseball players in the United States during World War II were men, and a good number of them had exchanged pin-striped uniforms and socks for army fatigues and boots. In 1942 Philip K. Wrigley, owner of the Chicago Cubs baseball team, got the idea to form a league of girl ballplayers called the All-American Girls Professional Baseball League.

Women had formed softball leagues in many cities across the United States, but women ballplayers were not professional. Wrigley changed that. He held auditions in dozens of cities, selecting the best players for his league. For many, the chance to play ball professionally was a dream come true. Many were teenagers, such as four-teen-year-old Dottie Schroeder. Schroeder was among the youngest players, so the older girls tried to help her both on and off the field.

The girls chosen, however, played by two sets of rules—rules of the game and rules of conduct. The game the girls played differed from men's baseball in a couple of ways. The ball was larger, about 12 inches (30 cm), though it got smaller in the years that followed. The pitches were underhand. The bats were lighter in weight, and the distances between the bases were shorter than in men's baseball.

The second set of rules governed the girls' behavior. First and foremost, the players had to appear ladylike. That meant, among other things, wearing a uniform that had a short skirt (just above the knee) rather than pants.

Appearance, however, extended far beyond the girls' uniforms. Each girl received a handbook that stressed "high moral standards." According to the handbook, the girls were always to remember that "your mind and your body are interrelated and you cannot neglect one without causing the other to suffer. A healthy mind and a healthy body are the true attributes of the All American girl."

Each player was issued a beauty kit so that she could be "at all times presentable and attractive." The kit included cleansing cream, lipstick, face powder, rouge, deodorant, hand lotion, and even a cream for hair removal. Rules of conduct stated that a girl must wear lipstick "at all times." Hair was a woman's "crowning glory," the handbook stated. And long hair was more glorious than "boyish bobs." The book provided directions for how to make the most of this crown of glory: brush daily. "Bend over," the book instructed, "and let your head hang down. Then brush your hair downward until the scalp tingles."

Rosie the Pinup Girl

The OWI liked the idea of pinup girls. These were patriotic posters of a different kind. Usually a Hollywood actress posed for a photograph wearing an elegant evening gown or something more revealing, such as a bathing suit. The photographs were then distributed to the soldiers overseas. They pinned these images on their lockers, in their bunks, or carried them in a backpack. Betty Grable's pose *(right)* was a real favorite. She is wearing a bathing suit and high heels and is standing with her back to the camera, her hands on her hips. Looking over her shoulder, she is smiling provocatively. Five million copies of that photograph landed in the hands of GIs. Said one soldier, "Suddenly someone sees her picture and we'd know what we were fighting for."

Pinup publicity photographs were a morale booster. But even pinups were "colored coded." African American GIs couldn't display Betty Grable on their bunks. Lena Horne *(left)* was the girl for them. Horne was an African American singer and actress. While there were dozens of beautiful white pinup girls, Horne was the first for the African American troops. She resented it, but not because a pinup girl was a romantic fantasy. She was an "afterthought," she said, "as if someone had suddenly turned to the Negro GIs and said: Oh, yes, here fellows, here's a pin up girl for you."

Above: *Actress, singer, and dancer Betty Grable was best-known for her shapely legs, which were showcased in all of her musicals and were insured by her movie studio for $2 million.*
Left: *Glamorous and talented Lena Horne appeared in a number of musicals. But she was never featured in a leading role, because films in which she appeared had to be re-edited for showing in southern states where theaters could not show films with African American performers.*

This aspect of the game was just as important as pitching, fielding, and batting abilities. After practicing all day on the field, the girls attended a charm school at night. Instructors from the Helena Rubinstein cosmetics company taught classes not only on how to apply makeup but also on how to speak clearly (enunciation) and how to stand, walk, and sit correctly (posture). After hours of squatting during practice, catcher Lovane Paire Davis, known as Pepper, often suffered leg cramps. No matter, she had to go to charm school. As Pepper recalled, "It wasn't easy to walk around in high heels with a book on your head when you had a charley horse."

Chaperones ensured that the girls followed the rules of conduct. If a girl came onto the field without lipstick, the chaperone told her about it. If a girl tried to sneak off for a date, the chaperone was right on her trail.

Because the All-American Girls Professional Baseball League required players to wear short skirts, sliding into base often resulted in badly cut or bruised legs. It happened so often that the girls had a name for these unsightly marks—strawberries.

At first, the American public was doubtful that the All-American Girls could play anything other than "glorified softball." Sports editors of newspapers, in particular, were skeptical that girls could provide fast action or thrilling plays. James F. Henderson, sports editor of the *Muskegon Chronicle* in Michigan, had his doubts. But he soon became a fan. "The girls do everything the men are asked to do," he wrote. "They field and throw, hit and run, make sensational catches, slide into bases recklessly, suffer painful injuries." Baseball was as American as apple pie, and so were baseball's Rosies. Although they played "rough" and gave everything to win "just like men," noted Henderson, they were still ladies. More than once, Henderson heard the fans (which numbered into the thousands) leaving the ballpark muttering, "Too bad they lost . . . but they're cute."

"Too bad they lost . . . but they're cute."

—a fan of the All-American Girls after a loss, 1947

Swinging with the USO

When asked what she planned to do after the war, musician Jane Sager would answer that she was going to do what she had done before the war—play trumpet. Sometimes the questioner would frown. That wasn't being patriotic, the frown suggested. Once the war ended, the women who had filled in temporarily for the men would give up their jobs and go home again. Even musicians.

The problem was that many women were earning a living or attempting to as musicians before the war. "We had a lot of pride in our work," Jane said, referring to female musicians in the 1930s. "We didn't want to sound crummy, because there was so much prejudice against women musicians to begin with."

Servicemen, servicewomen, and their families paid more than 12 million visits a month to United Service Organizations (USO) facilities during World War II. Here actress Marlene Dietrich talks with a group of U.S. servicemen on her USO visit to Vermont's Camp Meade.

The prejudice had to do with the type of instrument women traditionally played, and it wasn't horns or drums. When Peggy Gilbert was in high school, her boyfriend played saxophone in a band. One day she said, "Let me blow that horn, will you?" Once she did, she knew that she was going to play professionally. Her father objected. There were no saxophones in a symphony ,he reasoned. Peggy Gilbert had no intention of playing classical music with a symphony. She wanted to play with a swing band. "But you're a girl," he father told her.

In the 1920s and 1930s, women musicians rarely got the opportunity to play with male bands, and when they did, it was usually to play jazz piano. The guys just didn't think the girls were good enough. An article titled "Why Women Musicians Are Inferior" appeared in the February 1938 issue of *Downbeat* magazine. "It would seem that even though women are the weaker sex they would still be able to bring more out of a poor, defenseless horn than something that sounds like a cry for help," the article stated. Women musicians were too emotional to play well, and they were afraid that the facial contortions necessary to get power out of a horn would make them look silly. The author concluded, "Women are better performers on strings and piano, which are essentially sympathetic instruments more in keeping with their temperament."

Peggy Gilbert fired back a letter to the

editor of *Downbeat* magazine. "A woman has to be a thousand times more talented, has to have a thousand times more initiative even to be recognized as the peer of the least successful man. Why? Because of that age-old prejudice against women, that time-worn idea that women are the weaker sex, that women are innately inferior to men."

Faced with the prospect of not being allowed to play the type of music they loved, many women started their own all-girl bands. Peggy Gilbert's band was called the Dixie Belles. In 1936 a writer in the *Saturday Evening Post* bemoaned this

Help Wanted ads began to appear in music magazines, such as *Downbeat*, for girl musicians. But there was a hitch to this new opportunity. Talent was a necessary requirement. A girl had to be able to swing, play jazzy solos, or improvise (make up) music on the spot. But she also had to be attractive. That meant among other things, no eyeglasses (which made it hard for some girls to read music). All-girl bands were pinup girls with instruments, notes Sherrie Tucker, a professor of women's studies. The Help Wanted ad often asked the musicians to "send photo immediately."

"A woman has to be a thousand times more talented, has to have a thousand times more initiative even to be recognized as the peer of the least successful man."

—Peggy Gilbert, 1938

musical trend. "One more girl band is about all this country needs to send it right back into the depths of the Depression," he wrote. By 1941, however, the country couldn't get enough of the female musicians.

As in other professions, many male musicians had volunteered or were drafted into military service once the war began. Suddenly all-girl bands were being booked in ballrooms and theaters all across the country.

Would band leaders run an advertisement asking male musicians to submit a photograph? No, said Peggy Gilbert. Men got jobs based on their ability, not their good looks. Women were considered attractions. "And men like to look at attractive women," said Peggy. "The manager is continually reminding the girls not to take the music so seriously, but to relax, to smile. How can you smile with a horn in your mouth?"

It wasn't too easy to play the bass drum in high heels, either. But those were the special challenges women musicians faced.

During the war, this emphasis on attraction and femininity became even more important, especially if the girls were playing for the troops. Many all-girl bands toured with the United Service Organizations, or USO. In the United States, the USO had opened thousands of centers in cities across the country. The USO also toured army camps, both at home and overseas. When Joy Cayler and her All-Girl Orchestra played at Camp Polk, Louisiana, hundreds of soldiers stood in lines that wound across an open field. "American–style music and pretty girls" were real morale boosters. Band leader Ada Leonard, however, reminded her professional musicians, "Because you're a girl, people look at you first, then listen to you second."

The USO encouraged the all-girl bands to emphasize femininity. When performing onstage, the USO suggested, they ought to dress as if they were going on a Saturday night date with a special guy. To the soldiers, the girls onstage, often dressed in strapless gowns, were symbols of the sweethearts they had left behind.

"Because you're a girl, people look at you first, then listen to you second."

—band leader Ada Leonard, 1940s

Once the show began and the girls got swinging onstage, they changed a few minds about whether women musicians were inferior to men. The GIs responded with thunderous applause.

A Nurse First, A Woman Second

The motion picture begins with dramatic shots of combat somewhere in Europe. "Hang on," a voice tells a wounded soldier. The image on the screen blurs as the soldier slips in and out of consciousness. Medics transfer him by jeep away from the sounds of battle and toward the safety of a mobile hospital close behind the front lines. "When the dizziness

The Mystery of Tokyo Rose

Yet another Rose became a legend during World War II: "Hello there, Enemies! How's tricks? This is Ann of Radio Tokyo, and we're just going to begin our regular program of music, news and the *Zero Hour* for our friends—I mean, our enemies!—in Australia and the South Pacific."

"Ann" was a radio announcer working for the Japanese. Her program, called *Zero Hour*, broadcast American music to Australia and the islands of the South Pacific, where hundreds of thousands of U.S. soldiers were fighting for their lives. It was these soldiers who gave Ann the nickname Tokyo Rose.

The purpose of *Zero Hour* was to make U.S. soldiers homesick. Ann frequently teased them that while they were fighting in the mud and rain, their sweethearts back home were having a wonderful time dancing with new boyfriends. Some GIs thought her broadcasts were nonsense. Others thought she boosted rather than broke morale.

After the war ended, the U.S. Army arrested a Japanese American woman who had been living in Tokyo during the war and who was a broadcaster for Radio Tokyo. Iva Toguri *(right)* was a U.S. citizen.

Although Toguri denied being Tokyo Rose, the U.S. Army arrested her on October 17, 1945, and she spent nearly twelve months in a Tokyo prison. The army released her when it could not prove Toguri was indeed the infamous Rose. Her ordeal was not yet over, however. Upon her return to the United States, the Federal Bureau of Investigation (FBI) arrested her and charged her with treason. This time she was sentenced to ten years in prison.

The mystery about the identity of Tokyo Rose continued. Not until the 1970s, however, would the true story of Iva Toguri become known. The FBI had withheld evidence during the trial.

In 1977 President Gerald Ford pardoned Iva Toguri. She had become an old woman whose life had been destroyed by the prejudices of war. Despite her innocence, news headlines still linked her to the infamous Tokyo Rose. "FORD PARDONS TOYKO ROSE" suggested Toguri was indeed that fictitious character rather than a victim of war propaganda.

Patriotic exhibits stressed how important women were, both on the war front and on the home front. Without women's work, the United States could not win the war.

stopped and the fog lifted," the film's narrator states, "an Army Nurse was at your side. A woman who meant safety and comfort and home to thousands of men before you, a woman who meant all those things to you."

The Army Nurse was a recruiting film produced by the U.S. government in 1945. Although the end of the war seemed near, at least in Europe, the fighting continued. So, too, did the casualties. The need for trained military nurses had reached a critical point. The recruitment of military nurses was not as successful as the government had hoped. A WAC or a WAVE could be trained in a relatively short period of time. A nurse's medical education, however, took three years. The

government urged young women to enroll in nursing schools. But the immediate need for nurses meant that those already working in civilian hospitals across the country had to give up their jobs to enlist. Those who did had to undergo weeks of basic training, which included long hikes, exercises using gas masks, and other physical training to "toughen them up." Those who stuck it out received officer status. Some nurses worked on the home front in military hospitals. Many thousands of others traveled overseas, working in often harsh conditions in field hospitals or evacuation hospitals.

The Army Nurse recruitment film showed real nurses in real field hospital settings.

Meet Frances Bullock

OWI photographer Ann Rosener completed a series of photographs featuring Frances Bullock in various stages of becoming a nurse. The first photograph shows Frances at home in the bedroom, packing her suitcase. The caption reads: "Eager to be of service to her country, nineteen year old Frances Bullock prepares to leave her Lynchburg, Virginia home to enter one of the nation's 1,300 accredited schools of nursing."

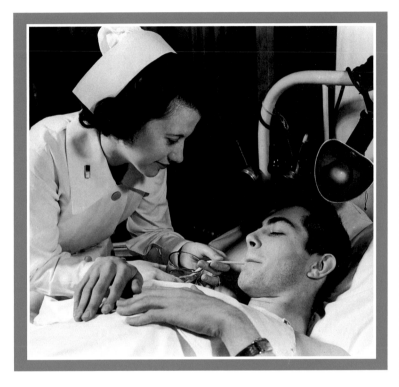

A second photograph showed Frances in an anatomy class, studying "the intricacies of brain structure." Because the purpose of the series was to encourage other young women to become nurses, a few photographs show Frances in a long evening dress, dancing with a young man. Nursing wasn't all work and no play, the caption explains. Nor were student nurses dull or homely. In subsequent photographs, Frances receives her cap. The capping ceremony usually happened midway through the first year of school. Frances "thrills" at her first operating room assignment. She graduates, becomes a Lieutenant Bullock and photographs show her (above) caring for wounded soldiers. She was a "modern Florence Nightingale" the caption read.

All the photographs on file in the government records are dated May 1943. Frances Bullock appears to have completed her studies in a single month. Ordinarily, the education and training of a nurse takes years, not weeks. Who was Frances Bullock? Was she another media creation, a patriotic symbol, like Rosie the Riveter? Frances might have been a real nurse. But the photographic series created by Ann Rosener for the OWI was a carefully planned media presentation.

She wore military fatigues, not the crisp, white uniform and cap of a civilian nurse. If her assignment was a mobile hospital—one that followed close behind the front lines—she often had to help pitch tents and set up surgical units. She slept on a cot in a tent, ate the same rations as he-soldiers, and often came under enemy fire. She hand washed her clothes in her helmet, as soldiers did.

Although the film didn't lie about the harsh conditions, it nevertheless glorified the nurse's call to duty. She did not work for wages but rather "to ease the pain of war, to help save lives." "It's the surgeon who saves a man's life; it's the nurse whose tender care helps him to live," the narrator stated. "In her is the tenderness of all women—of mother and sister and friend. . . . She works with her head, her hands, and her heart. . . . She is a nurse first, a woman second, and an officer third."

Despite the government's recruitment efforts, the need for nurses was so critical in 1945 that President Roosevelt considered drafting civilian nurses into military service. Civilian hospitals in the United States on the average had one nurse for every twelve patients. Military hospitals, however, had only one nurse for every twenty-six patients. Complicating the problem was the fact that many military nurses were themselves being hospitalized, due to stress and overwork. If nurses did not enlist voluntarily, then the president could see no other way to solve the problem. "The need is too pressing to await the outcome of further efforts at recruiting," he said.

"We will have our men cared for," echoed Congresswoman Frances Bolton.

The president never asked Congress to establish a draft of women nurses into the military. But the possibility of such an event triggered a barrage of letters to the editors of

Recruitment posters for the U.S. Army Nurse Corps showed beautifully made-up young women in uniform.

The real life of nurses sent off to combat zones did not involve dress uniforms, well-coiffed hair, or even the respect that their rank should have commanded. The nurse above prepares to fly with a wounded U.S. soldier as he is evacuated in the 1940s from Guadalcanal in the Solomon Islands.

newspapers and magazines. These letters helped to explain why American nurses were not answering the call of their country. It had little to do with patriotism or glamour.

The reasons were many. Some nurses disliked being ordered around by women officers with less medical experience. Others objected to the physical requirements of basic training, with its grueling calisthenics and close-order drills. They were nurses, not soldiers.

The primary reason, however, was a resentment of having to do clerical or routine tasks that required little medical experience, such as making beds, typing reports, emptying bedpans. They especially disliked "kitchen patrol," or KP duty. Even though the propaganda posters and films claimed she was a nurse first and a woman second, in reality, some nurses found the opposite to be true. The military treated her as a woman first and a nurse second. "We know we're needed and we willingly lend all our support," wrote one military nurse. "But . . . give me some real nursing, instead of K.P. for the duration."

Another reason for the shortage of nurses was related to the dangers of military nursing. Hundreds of nurses had died overseas, and many more had been taken prisoner. Even in relatively safe locations, working conditions were challenging. A group of twelve registered nurses wrote a letter to *Time* in which they stated why they would not enlist. Their brothers, sweethearts, and friends who were soldiers overseas had written to them that war is no place for a lady.

Nurse Helen Baird Rapuzzi read that letter and disagreed. She wrote to *Time* as well. "I say [war's] no place for anyone but a lady."

Even after four years of war, even after millions of dollars spent to convince

The Japanese did not surrender.

On the morning of August 6, 1945, air-raid sirens wailed in the Japanese city of Hiroshima. A few minutes later, a few people spotted high above what seemed to be a heavy airplane bomber. What happened next would shock the world. In a flash of blinding light, followed by a scalding, hurricane-like wind, Hiroshima was destroyed. The United States had dropped the first of two atomic bombs on

"I say [war's] no place for anyone but a lady."

—Nurse Helen Baird Rapuzzi, 1945

Americans that women "could do it," even after millions of women had gone to work and proven that they "had done it," the debate about masculine and feminine abilities continued. Neither the war nor the propaganda campaigns had swept away the stereotypes about a woman's place in society.

"Rain of Ruin"

Harry S. Truman became president after the death of Franklin Roosevelt in April 1945. That summer he warned the Japanese government of a new weapon the United States had developed. If Japan did not surrender, it would experience "a rain of ruin from the air, the likes of which had never been seen on earth."

Japan. Never before had atomic power been unleashed, and the destruction was appalling. Approximately 200,000 people died. Many thousands more suffered from radiation burns caused by the blast's atomic wind.

Three days later, another atomic bomb destroyed Nagasaki. Soon after, Japan's Emperor Hirohito surrendered unconditionally. World War II was over.

So, too, was a way of life. The OWI posters disappeared. The war factories shut down. Millions, though not all, American working women went home. But life had changed, not just for women and not just for other Americans. The tremors of the two atomic explosions shook the world. People had seen what atomic weapons could do.

Battered religious figures stand watch on a hill above a tattered valley after the atomic bomb devastated Nagasaki, Japan, on August 9, 1945.

They began to fear what those weapons could do again—destroy not just a city but a country.

"Seldom if ever has a war ended leaving the victors with such a sense of uncertainty and fear, with such a realization that the future is obscure and that survival is not assured," radio journalist Edward R. Murrow said.

The media gave a name to America's new anxiety: the Cold War (1945–1991). The country was at peace, and yet the threat of war seemed to rumble like an echo in the distance. The enemy was the Soviet Union, a Communist country in Europe. Within a few years, the Soviet Union would begin testing its own atomic weapons. Americans feared the Communists would use the atomic bomb to start a third world war. "We must be prepared for the worst!" the military warned the nation. The days of the Cold War had begun.

Mrs. America goes home

A LITTLE LUXURY YOU'VE EARNED . . . .

Elizabeth Arden
SOAPS
FRESH   FRAGRANT   LASTING

*After the war,
I could never go back to playing bridge again,
being a club woman . . . when I knew there were
things you could use your mind for.*

—Inez Sauer, Boeing tool clerk, 1940s

In the 1930s, while First Lady Eleanor Roosevelt was traveling

about the country as First Lady and reporting to her husband about what she had seen, she received a letter from a woman who had just visited the White House. It stated: "Instead of tearing around the country, I think you should stay at home and personally see that the White House is clean. I soiled my white gloves yesterday morning on the stair-railing. It is disgraceful."

The letter writer was not criticizing the White House staff for doing a sloppy job. Rather, she was offended by the nontraditional role Mrs. Roosevelt had taken as First Lady. A woman's place was in the home, even if that home was the White House.

When Franklin Roosevelt died in the spring of 1945, Eleanor Roosevelt packed her belongings and returned to her home in New York. The new First Lady, Bess Truman, was more traditional. She ended the Monday morning press conferences. She did not write her own news column or magazine articles. She did not travel about the country investigating social conditions.

The change in the White House reflected a change in the United States. In the 1930s, during the Great Depression, women faced scorn and ridicule if they took a job from a man. During the war years, the government aggressively changed the country's perception of working women—they were necessary, and they were capable. A woman could work and still be feminine. After the war, the message was once again that women's purpose in life, at least during peacetime, was to become a wife and a mother.

This change in attitude had begun even before the war ended. "A woman doing war work in slacks is a woman right now dreaming of going back to her life as a woman at home," wrote Jean Austin, the editor of the *American Home* magazine in October 1942.

Were all women dreaming that same dream? Not likely. Government surveys conducted in 1944 concluded that as many as 80 percent of the women working during the war hoped to keep their jobs after the war. But that did not happen. As soldiers returned home, employers laid off their female workers. Some Rosies quit, no doubt because they wanted to become full-time mothers and wives again. Others, however, quit because popular culture pressured them to do so.

"Back to School—Back to Work" was the title of a magazine advertisement for Phillips' Milk of Magnesia. The illustrations showed a man in a business suit and a boy about ten years old rushing out the front door. The man carries a briefcase. The boy carries his books. Standing in the doorway and waving good-bye with a smile on her face is Mom. Even the dog is running out the door, but the woman must stay at home.

Advertisements in women's magazines

changed. Gone were the safety goggles and lunch pails. Gone were the work shirts and overalls. Women appeared most often as Mrs. America, the housewife and mother. Fashion designer Christian Dior declared a "New Look" in women's clothing. Skirts were longer. Waists were nipped. Women once more looked like women instead of laborers.

Palmolive once again sold its soap by featuring frustrated young ladies who didn't understand why they didn't have dates. "If you want a complexion the envy of every woman—the admiration of every man—start the 14-Day Palmolive Plan tonight!"

Palmolive's postwar campaign most often showed women in social situations, at picnics or sleigh riding, for example. On occasion, an advertisement pictured a woman at work in an office. She, too, is frustrated. She complains to her coworker, who sits at a typewriter, "Watch the promotions go by! Honestly, I'll be a file clerk for the rest of my life if I don't find a way to fix up this dull, dingy complexion of mine!"

Rosies most likely to keep their jobs during the postwar years were those in traditionally female occupations, such as nurses, teachers, or secretaries. The filing clerk in Palmolive's advertisement could wash her face for months, even years, and still not remove the social stereotypes that limited her employment opportunities. She might get a

At the end of World War II, women were once again regarded by the media as fragile, feminine creatures centered on home and family. But was it working? Or was Rosie still lurking under her perfect complexion?

promotion to typist or even personal secretary. But facial soap would never land her such important decision-making positions as executive officer or vice president.

Babies, too, began appearing in advertisements for soap, food, and medical products. Always a woman, never a man, cuddled, fed, and played with these promotional cherubs. Short stories and Hollywood movies presented women as Mrs. Americas. Even Annie Oakley, the sharpshooter in the Broadway musical *Annie Get Your Gun* (1946), longs to become the wife of Frank Butler. Frank knows what he wants in a wife.

In Act I, Frank sings about the girl that he'll marry. She'll be "as soft and as pink as a nursery." That's not all. She'll dress in "satins and laces and smell of cologne" and instead of "flittin'" she'll sit and "purr like a kitten."

Annie wears buckskins instead of satins. She, too, sings a few songs in this Broadway musical. One is called "I Can Do Anything Better Than You." Annie can certainly outshoot Frank, but she'd gladly give it up to be his wife. *Annie Get Your Gun* was a big hit in the postwar years and later made into an equally popular Hollywood movie.

Annie Oakley apparently found it easy to adjust to being a wife and mother. In real life, going home again presented problems, especially for the soldiers who had suffered the trauma of war. Women, too, often found it difficult to adjust to changing times. Divorce rates increased. A government "readjustment" guide provided advice to the new Mrs. America learning how to get along once again with their husbands. "Let him know you are tired of living alone. . . . You want him to take charge. You want now to have your nails done."

Some women, both fictional and real, survived. Brenda Starr, the comic-book heroine born in the 1940s, would continue to uncover and fight evil in the world for many more decades to come. Some women did get those promotions, and not just to typist or office manager. In the decades to come, women would become leaders in the civil rights movement. They would win election to the House and Senate. They would write books that challenged science and crushed social stereotypes.

Ah, but their stories—Rosa Parks's, Margaret Chase Smith's, Rachel Carson's, and others—are the stuff of Book 4, *Gidgets and Women Warriors.*

Source Notes

6 "Eleanor Everywhere," *Time*, November 20, 1933, n.d., http://www.time.com/time/magazine/article/0,9171,929575-5,00.html (March 1, 2007).

7 Eleanor Roosevelt, *This I Remember* (New York: Harper & Brothers, 1949), 74.

8 Ibid.

8 Joseph P. Lash, *Eleanor and Franklin* (New York: W. W. Norton, 1971), 355.

13 Samuel Crowther, "What You Can Do," *Ladies' Home Journal*, March 1932, 3.

15 "The King Speaks," *Library of Congress*, January 7, 1932, image LC-USZ62-126679, n.d., http://www.loc.gov/rr/print/swann/blondie/object.html#Repro (February 15, 2007).

16 *Time*, "Blondie's Father," May 9, 1949, n.d., http://www.time.com/time/magazine/article/0,9171,800248,00.html (February 6, 2007).

20 Edythe Meserand, interview by the Washington Press Club Foundation, August 31, 1990, *WPCF*, n.d., http://64.70.191.96/wpforal/mes.htm (February 6, 2007).

20 Ibid.

22 John Dunning, *On the Air: The Encyclopedia of Old-Time Radio* (New York: Oxford University Press, 1998), 332.

24 *Time*, "The Lady Is Insecure," September 12, 1949, n.d., http://www.time.com/time/magazine/article/0,9171,888642,00.html (February 6, 2007).

32 Jeanine Basinger, *A Woman's View: How Hollywood Spoke to Women 1930–1960* (Middleton, CT: Wesleyan University Press, 1993), 18.

38 Ibid., 4.

38 Ibid., 24.

40 Thomas Doherty, *Pre-Code Hollywood: Sex, Immorality and Insurrection in America Cinema, 1930–1934* (New York: Columbia University Press, 1999), 64.

40 *Time*, "Again, Boop," April 30, 1934, n.d., http://www.time.com/time/magazine/article/0,9171,930479,00.html (February 6, 2007).

42 Margaret Farrand Thorp, *America at the Movies* (New Haven, CT: Yale University Press, 1939), 205–206.

44 Gary Arnold, "Shirley Temple: Curly-Haired Moppet Lifted Spirits of a Depression Nation," *Washington Times*, December 6, 1998.

50 *Time*, Obituary, February 10, 1961, n.d., http://www.time.com/time/magazine/article/0,9171,872153,00.html (February 6, 2007).

50 Richard Corliss, "Anna May Wong Did It Right," *Time*, January 29, 2005, n.d., http://www.time.com/time/columnist/corliss/article/0,9565,1022536,00.html (February 6, 2007).

52 Gerald Peary, "Righting Wong," Boston Phoenix, March 19-25, 2004, http://bostonphoenix.com/boston/movies/film/documents/03678230.asp (April 3, 2007).

53 Graham Russell Gao Hodges, *Anna May Wong: From Laundryman's Daughter to Hollywood Legend* (New York: Palgrave Macmillan, 2004), 167.

53 Ibid., 19.

57 *Vogue*, "A Catastrophe? Or a Blessing?" January 4, 1930, 67.

57 Ibid.

58 *New York Times*, "70% of Hunter Girls Rebel at Long Skirts," November 25, 1929, 23.

58 *New York Times*, "Osteopaths Favor 'Freedom' in Dress," March 24, 1929, 19.

58 *New York Times*, "Talks Fail to Fix Length of Skirts," December 13, 1929, 36.

60 "Vogue's-Eye View of the Mode," January 15, 1930, "They Wore America on Their Sleeves," *American Studies at the University of Virginia*, n.d., http://xroads.virginia.edu/~MA04/hess/Fashion/vogue/02_1930_1.pdf (February 15, 2007).

62 "How's Your Breath Today?" Listerine, *Vanity Fair*, May 1933, n.d., http://xroads.virginia.edu/~1930s/PRINT/vanity/chaptwo.html (February 15, 2007) .

64 Margaret Culkin Banning, "Three Sides to a Charge Account," *Ladies' Home Journal*, March 1933, 17.

64 Crowther, 3.

64 *Ladies' Home Journal*, "The Tragedy of Nan—Domestic Hands," March 1932, 85.

65 *Nation*, "These Modern Women," March 16, 1927, available online at "Revues and other Vanities: The Commodification of Fantasy in the 1920s," *Assumption College*, n.d., http://www.assumption .edu/ahc/Vanities (February 6, 2007).

67 *Time*, "Channel Crossing," August 16, 1926, n.d., http://www.time.com/time/printout/0,8816,722331 ,00.html (February 6, 2007).

68 Bobbie Rosenfeld, "Feminine Sports Reel," *Globe and Mail*, January 10, 1941, available online at *Jewish Women's Archives*, n.d., http://www.jwa.org/ teach/primarysources/news_02.pdf (February 6, 2007).

68 Paul Gallico, "Don't Flatter Yourselves, Girls," *The World in Vogue*, edited by Bryan Holme, Katharine Tweed, Jessica Daves, and Alexander Liberman (New York: Viking Press, 1963), 150.

68 Anne Marie Pippin, "From Muscle Moll to Queen of the Greens," n.d., http://www.uga.edu/juro/2003/ pippin.htm (February 6, 2007).

69 Gallico, 149–150.

70 *Time*, "Tomboy Turns Pro," November 25, 1940, n.d., http://www.time.com/time/magazine/article/ 0,9171,884157,00.html (February 6, 2007).

72 Don Congdon, ed. *The Thirties: A Time to Remember* (New York: Simon and Schuster, 1962), 75.

73 Ibid., 74.

73 Ibid.

77 William B. Breuer, *War and American Women: Heroes, Deeds, and Controversy* (New York: Praeger, 1997), 14.

77 Ruth Cowan Nash, interview by Washington Press Club Foundation, September 26, 1987, *WPCF*, n.d., http://64.70.191.96/wpforal/rcn.htm (February 6, 1007).

78 Maurine Hoffman Beasley, *Eleanor Roosevelt and the Media: A Public Quest for Self-Fulfillment* (Urbana: University of Illinois Press, 1987), 38.

80 Richard Lowitt and Maurine Beasley. *One Third of a Nation: Lorena Hickok Reports from the Great Depression* (Urbana: University of Illinois Press, 1981), xxviii.

82 Daedalus Howell, "Starr Gazer," *Sonoma County Independent*, February 19–25, 1998, Reprinted

online, n.d., http://www.metroactive.com/papers/ sonoma/02.19.98/comics-9807.html (February 15, 2007).

83 *Time*, "Man in a Woman's World," January 6, 1947, n.d., http://www.time.com/time/magazine/article/ 0,9171,853046,00.html (February 6, 2007).

83 *Time*, "Best Man in the Business," October 6, 1941, n.d., http://www.time.com/time/magazine/article/ 0,9171,790290,00.html (February 6, 2007).

83 Ibid.

84 William Stott, *Documentary Expression and Thirties America* (New York: Oxford University Press, 1973), 29.

85 Dorothea Lange, "The Assignment I'll Never Forget," *Popular Photography*, February 1960, 42–43.

86 Margaret Bourke-White, *Portrait of Myself* (New York: Simon and Schuster, 1963), 110.

87 Ibid.

88 Frances Perkins, "The Roots of Social Security," *Social Security Online*, n.d., http://www.ssa.gov/history/ perkins5.html (February 6, 2007).

89 *Time*, "Eleanor Everywhere," November 20, 1933, n.d., http://www.time.com/time/magazine/article/ 0,9171,929575,00.html (February 6, 2007).

89 Ruth de Forest Lamb, *American Chambers of Horrors* (New York: Farrar & Rinehart, 1936), 327.

90 Ibid., 33.

90 Ibid., 29.

91 Ibid., 33–34.

92 Ibid., 3.

97 Ibid., 341.

98 Eleanor Roosevelt, letter, February 26, 1939, n.d., http://www.fdrlibrary.marist.edu/restxt.html (February 15, 2007).

100 Sheridan Harvey, "Rosie the Riveter: Real Women Workers in World War II," *Journeys and Crossings*, Library of Congress, August 1, 2006, http://www.loc .gov/rr/program/journey/rose-transcript.html (March 2, 2007).

106 "The Price of Liberty," U.S. Department of Defense in cooperation with the Council of Motion Picture Organizations, 1951, *Internet Archive*, n.d., http://www.archive.org/details/price_of_liberty (February 15, 2007).

108 "Loretta Young Trailer, 1941/11/23," Universal News Reels (Hollywood, CA: Universal Studios) *Internet Archive*, n.d., http://www.archive.org/details/1942-11 -23_Loretta_Young_Trailer (February 15, 2007).

110 Sheridan Harvey, "Real Women Workers in World War II," *Library of Congress*, n.d., http://www.loc.gov/rr/program/journey/rosie -transcript.html (February 6, 2007).

112 Maureen Honey, *Creating Rosie the Riveter: Class, Gender, and Propaganda during World War II* (Amherst: University of Massachusetts Press, 1984), 126.

115 *Library of Congress American Memory*, n.d., http://lcweb2.loc.gov/cgi-bin/query/D?ils:1:./temp/ ~pp_NkyQ::@@@mdb=fsaall (April 5, 2007).

115 Stanley Frank and Paul Sann, "Paper Dolls," *Saturday Evening Post*, May 23, 1944, 20–21.

116 Emily Yellin, *Our Mother's War: American Women at Home and at the Front during World War II* (New York: Simon and Schuster, 2004), 112.

116 Ibid., 218.

118 Jack Fincher, "'The Belles of the Ball Game' Were a Hit with their Fans," *Smithsonian*, July 1989, 88–97.

119 James F. Henderson, "A New American Sport," 1947 *Muskegon Lassies yearbook,* reprinted at All-American Girls Professional Baseball League, 2005, http://www.aagpbl.org/articles/general.cfm?ID=8 (February 6, 2007).

120 Sherry Tucker, *Swing Shift: All Girl Bands of the 1940s* (Durham, NC: Duke University Press, 2000), 49.

120 Peggy Gilbert, *The Smithsonian Jazz Oral History Program*, n.d., http://www.si.edu/ajazzh/johp.htm (February 15, 2007).

121 Robert Walser, ed., *Keeping Time: Readings in Jazz History* (New York: Oxford University Press, 1999), 112.

121 Ibid., 116.

122 Ibid., 112.

122 Tucker, 49.

122 Ibid., 230.

125 Signal Corps, "The Army Nurse," (Washington, DC: U.S. Army Pictorial Service, 1945).

127 *Time*, "Draft Women?" January 15, 1945, n.d., http://www.time.com/time/magazine/article/ 0,9171,775362,00.html (February 6, 1007).

127 *Time*, "Where Are the Nurses," November 20, 1944, n.d., http://www.time.com/time/magazine/article/ \0,9171,796818,00.html (February 6, 2007).

128 *Time*, Letters, March 7, 1945, n.d., http://www.time.com/time/magazine/article/ 0,9171,797451,00.html (February 6, 2007).

128 Ibid., May 28, 1945, n.d., http://www.time.com/time/printout/0,8816,775630 ,00.html (February 6, 2007).

130 Pat Kaufma, "Rosie the Riveter Remembers," *Organization of American Historians Magazine of History* 16:3, Spring 2002, 25.

131 Roosevelt, 92.

131 Charles Lewis and John Neville, "Images of Rosie: A Content Analysis of Women Workers in American Magazine Advertising, 1940–1946," *Journalism and Mass Communications Quarterly*, Spring 1995, 220.

133 Betsy Israel, *Bachelor Girl: 100 Years of Breaking the Rules—a Social History of Living Single* (New York: Harper Collins Publishers, 2002), 149.

Selected Bibliography

Adam, C. C. *The Best War Ever.* Baltimore: John Hopkins University Press, 1993.

Allen, Frederick Lewis. *The Big Change.* New York: Harper and Brothers, 1942.

Anderson, Marian. *My Lord What a Morning: An Autobiography.* New York: Viking Press, 1956.

Andriest, Ralph K. *The American Heritage History of the 1920s & 1930s.* New York: American Heritage Pub. Co., 1970.

Arnold, Gary. "Shirley Temple: Curly-Haired Moppet Lifted Spirits of a Depression Nation," *Washington Times*, December 6, 1998, 1.

Banning, Margaret Culkin, "Ask Your Purse," *Ladies' Home Journal*, May, 1936, 19.

Basinger, Jeanine. *A Woman's View: How Hollywood Spoke to Women 1930–1960.* Middleton, CT: Wesleyan University Press, 1993.

Beasley, Maurine Hoffman. *Eleanor Roosevelt and the Media: A Public Quest for Self-Fulfillment.* Urbana: University of Illinois Press, 1987.

Belford, Barbara. *Brilliant Bylines: A Biographical Anthology of Notable Newspaperwomen in America.* New York: Columbia University Press, 1986.

Best, Gary Dean. *The Nickel and Dime Decade: American Popular Culture during the 1930s.* Westport, CT: Praeger Publishers, 1993.

Bourke-White, Margaret. *Portrait of Myself.* New York: Simon and Schuster, 1963.

Brumberg, Joan Jacobs. *The Body Project: An Intimate History of American Girls.* New York: Random House, 1997.

Buck, Pearl S. *My Several Worlds.* New York: John Day Company, 1954.

Congdon, Don, ed. *The Thirties: A Time to Remember.* New York: Simon and Schuster, 1962.

Corliss, Richard. "Anna May Wong Did It Right," *Time*, January 29, 2005. N.d. http://www.time.com/time/columnist/corliss/article/0,9565,1022536,00.html

(February 15, 2007).

Duke University. *Emergence of Advertising in America, 1850–1920.* Rare Book, Manuscript, and Special Collections Library, Duke University. N.d. http://scriptorium.lib.duke.edu/eaa/ (February 15, 2007).

Dunning, John. *On the Air: The Encyclopedia of Old-Time Radio.* New York: Oxford University Press, 1998.

Fincher, Jack. "'The Belles of the Ball Game' Were a Hit with Their Fans," *Smithsonian*, July 1989, 88–97.

Frank, Stanley, and Paul Sann. "Paper Dolls." *Saturday Evening Post*, May 23, 1944, 20+.

Gallico, Paul. "Don't Flatter Yourselves, Girls." In Bryan Holme, Katharine Tweed, Jessica Daves, and Alexander Liberman, eds. *The World in Vogue.* New York: Viking Press, 1963.

Gordon, Herbert, "Women Are Writing the News!" *Christian Science Monitor*, September 25, 1943, 5.

Gregory, G. H., ed. *Posters of World War II.* New York: Gramercy Books, 1993.

Halper, Donna L. *Invisible Stars: A Social History of Women in American Broadcasting.* Armonk, NY: M. E. Sharpe, 2001.

Harris, Theodore F. and Pearl S. Buck. *Pearl S. Buck: A Biography.* New York: John Day Company, 1969.

Hodges, Graham Russell Gao. *Anna May Wong: From Laundryman's Daughter to Hollywood Legend.* New York: Palgrave Macmillan, 2004.

Honey, Maureen. *Creating Rosie the Riveter: Class, Gender, and Propaganda during World War II.* Amherst: University of Massachusetts Press, 1984.

Hosley, David H., and Gayle K. Yamada. *Hard News: Women in Broadcast Journalism.* Westport, CT: Greenwood Press, 1987.

Howell, Daedalus, "Starr Gazer," *Sonoma County Independent*, February 19–25, 1998.

Israel, Betsy. *Bachelor Girl: 100 Years of Breaking the Rules—a Social History of Living Single.* New York: Harper Collins Publishers, 2002.

Kennedy, David. *Freedom from Fear: The American People in Depression and War, 1929–1945.* New York: Oxford University Press, 1999.

Lamb, Ruth de Forest. *American Chambers of Horrors.* New York: Farrar & Rinehart, 1936.

Landay, Lori. *Madcaps, Screwballs, Con Women: The Female Trickster in American Culture.* Philadelphia: University of Pennsylvania Press, 1998.

Lange, Dorothea, "The Assignment I'll Never Forget," *Popular Photography,* February 1960, 42–43.

Lash, Joseph P. *Eleanor and Franklin.* New York: W. W. Norton, 1971.

Lewis, Charles, and John Neville. "Images of Rosie: A Content Analysis of Women Workers in American Magazine Advertising, 1940–1946." *Journalism and Mass Communications Quarterly,* Spring 1995, 216–227.

Lowe, Margaret A. *Looking Good: College Women and Body Image: 1875–1930.* Baltimore: Johns Hopkins University Press, 2003.

Lowitt, Richard, and Maurine Beasley. *One Third of a Nation: Lorena Hickok Reports from the Great Depression.* Urbana: University of Illinois Press, 1981.

Lutz, R. R. *Women Works and Labor Supply.* New York: National Industrial Conference Board, 1936.

Lynd, Robert S., and Helen Merrill Lynd. *Middletown in Transition: A Study in Cultural Conflicts.* New York: Harcourt, Brace and Co., 1937.

Palmer, Phyllis. *Domesticity and Dirt: Housewives and Domestic Servants in the U.S., 1920–1945.* Philadelphia: Temple University Press, 1989.

Phillips, Cabel. *From the Crash to the Blitz: 1929–1939.* New York: Macmillan Co., 1969.

Riordan, Teresa. *Inventing Beauty.* New York: Broadway Books, 2004.

Rogers, Agnes. *I Remember Distinctly: A Family Album of the American People, 1918–1941.* New York: Harper & Brothers Publishers, 1947.

Roosevelt, Eleanor. "Keepers of Democracy." *Virginia Quarterly Review,* Winter 1939 1–5.

——. *This I Remember.* New York: Harper & Brothers, 1949.

Ross, Ishbel. *Ladies of the Press.* New York: Harper & Brothers, 1936.

Scharf, Lois, and Joan M. Jensen. *Decades of Discontent: The Women's Movement, 1920–1940.* Westport, CT: Greenwood Press, 1983.

Stott, William. *Documentary Expression and Thirties America.* New York: Oxford University Press, 1973.

Thaggert, Miriam. "Divided Images: Black Female Spectatorship and John Stahl's 'Imitation of Life,'" *African American Review,* Fall 1998, 481–491.

Thorp, Margaret Farrand. *America at the Movies.* New Haven, CT: Yale University Press, 1939.

Time, "Skirted: Exclusion of Women from White House Correspondent's Dinner," March 13, 1944. N.d. http://www.time.com/time/magazine/article/ 0,9171,932424,00.html (February 15, 2007).

Time-Life Books. *This Fabulous Century: Sixty Years of American Life.* Vol. 4. New York: Time-Life Books, 1969.

Tucker, Sherry. *Swing Shift: All Girl Bands of the 1940s.* Durham, NC: Duke University Press, 2000.

Van Derman, Ruth. "11 O'clock, the White House," *Smith Alumnae Quarterly,* November 1935. N.d. http://saqonline.smith.edu/article.epl?issue_id =16&article_id=332 (February 15, 2007).

Walser, Robert, ed. *Keeping Time: Readings in Jazz History.* New York: Oxford University Press, 1999.

Watkins, T. H. *The Hungry Years.* New York: Henry Holt and Co., 1999.

Williams, Carol Traynor. *"It's Time for My Story": Soap Opera Sources, Structure, and Response.* Westport, CT: Praeger, 1992.

Yellin, Emily. *Our Mother's War: American Women at Home and at the Front during World War II.* New York: Simon and Schuster, 2004.

Further Reading and Websites

BOOKS

Brumberg, Joan Jacobs. *The Body Project: An Intimate History of American Girls.* New York: Random House, 1997.

Collins, Gail. *America's Women: 400 Years of Dolls, Drudges, Helpmates, and Heroines.* New York: William Morrow, 2003.

Deutsh, Sarah Jane. *From Breadlines to Ballots: American Women 1920–1940.* New York: Oxford University Press, 1994.

Douglas, Susan J. *Where the Girls Are: Growing Up Female with the Mass Media.* New York: Times Books, 1995.

Ferris, Jeri. *What I Had Was Singing: The Story of Marian Anderson.* Minneapolis: Twenty-First Century Books, 1994.

Goldstein, Margaret J. *World War II: Europe.* Minneapolis: Twenty-First Century Books, 2004.

Gourley, Catherine. *War, Women and the News: How Female Journalists Won the Battle to Cover World War II.* New York: Atheneum Press, 2007.

Halper, Donna L. *Invisible Stars: A Social History of Women in American Broadcasting.* New York: M. E. Sharpe, 2001.

Keller, Emily. *Margaret Bourke-White: A Photographer's Life.* Minneapolis: Twenty-First Century Books, 1996.

Kuhn, Betsy. *Angels of Mercy: The Army Nurses of World War II.* New York: Atheneum Books for Young Readers, 1999.

Matthews, Glenna. *American Women's History, A Student Companion.* New York: Oxford University Press, 2000.

Miller, Brandon Marie. *Dressed for the Occasion: What Americans Wore, 1620–1970.* Minneapolis: Twenty-First Century Books, 1999.

Riordan, Teresa. *Inventing Beauty.* New York: Broadway Books, 2004.

Sheer, Lynn, and Jurate Kazickas. *Susan B. Anthony Slept Here: A Guide to American Women's Landmarks.* New York: Times Books, 1994.

Whitman, Sylvia. *Uncle Sam Wants You! Military Men and Women of World War II.* Minneapolis: Twenty-First Century Books, 1993.

Williams, Barbara. *World War II: Pacific.* Minneapolis: Twenty-First Century Books, 2005.

Winget, Mary. *Eleanor Roosevelt.* Minneapolis: Twenty-First Century Books, 2001.

WEBSITES

Advertisements

The Ad*Access Project
http://scriptorium.lib.duke.edu/adaccess
This is a project of the Rare Book, Manuscript, and Special Collections Library, Duke University. The site has more than seven thousand advertisements that were printed in U.S. and Canadian newspapers and magazines between 1911 and 1955. The main subject categories are Beauty and Hygiene, Radio, Television, Transportation, and World War II.

Medicine and Madison Avenue
http://scriptorium.lib.duke.edu/mma/
This website has a database of more than six hundred health-related advertisements printed in newspapers and magazines between 1911 and 1958. It includes Instructor's and Student's Guides to provide ideas for use of the database in the classroom.

Magazine Cover Art

MagazineArt.org
http://www.magazineart.org
This site features color images from hundreds of magazines published in the nineteenth and early twentieth centuries. Also provided is information about magazines, their publishers, editors, artists, and publishing companies.

Music and Film

Jitterbuzz.com

http://www.jitterbuzz.com
This site provides the sounds and sights of the swing and jazz eras, from the 1920s through the 1950s. Listen to music, learn about artifacts (such as old telephones and radios), and read articles about music, film, and the people who created them.

Society and Social Customs

America in the 1930s

http://xroads.virginia.edu
The American Studies program at the University of Virginia provides an online resource of images and articles on daily life and popular culture of the 1930s. Download images and excerpts from magazines, film, and radio, as well as news articles.

The American Museum of Photography

http://www.photographymuseum.com
This award-winning Virtual Museum includes five thousand individual images, from the earliest daguerreotype portraits to the work of Ansel Adams.

National Museum of American History

http://americanhistory.si.edu/collections
This site provides a searchable database of exhibitions covering many of the topics touched upon in this book, including fashions, working women, and war posters. The site includes oral histories, prints, photographs, and drawings.

They Wore America on Their Sleeves

http://xroads.virginia.edu/~MA04/hess/Fashion/theyworeamericahome.html
This website, also sponsored by the American Cultures project at the University of Virginia, provides information on the relationship between clothes and society. Primary source documents digitalized online include news articles and catalog pages.

War

The World War II Poster Collection
http://www.library.northwestern.edu/govinfo/collections/wwii-posters
The Government and Geographic Information and Data Services Department at Northwestern University Library has a comprehensive collection of more than three hundred posters issued by U.S. government agencies during World War II.

Index

Photo Acknowledgments

The images in this book are used with the permission of:

© Bettmann/CORBIS, pp. 3, 17, 30, 38, 67 (left), 75, 96; "MR. SMITH GOES TO WASHINGTON", © 1939, renewed 1967 Columbia Pictures Industries, Inc., All Rights Reserved, Courtesy of Columbia Pictures, Image provided by The Kobal Collection, p. 4; National Archives, pp. 6, 86, 99 (right), 101, 103 (top), 105 (right), 107, 109, 111 (right), 112, 114 (all), 126, 127, 129; Franklin D. Roosevelt Library, pp. 8, 10 (top), 80, 88; The Cradle of Aviation Museum, p. 9; Library of Congress, pp. 10 (bottom), 19, 20, 46, 51, 67 (right), 68, 70 (both), 71, 74, 84, 85, 93, 97, 103 (middle and bottom), 104 (both), 105 (left), 111 (left), 125; Image courtesy of The Advertising Archives, pp. 12, 130; A DAMSEL IN DISTRESS © RKO Pictures, Inc. Licensed by Warner Bros. Entertainment Inc. All Rights Reserved, p. 14; BLONDIE © KING FEATURES SYNDICATE, Image courtesy of the Library of Congress, p. 15; © Schenectady Museum; Hall of Electrical History Foundation/CORBIS, p. 22; © Getty Images, pp. 23, 29, 31, 32, 41, 54, 59 (both), 72, 99 (left), 117 (bottom), 120; Library of American Broadcasting, University of Maryland, p. 24; © Brown Brothers, pp. 26, 27, 28, 47, 79; GOLD DIGGERS OF 1933 © Turner Entertainment Co. A Warner Bros. Entertainment Company. All Rights Reserved. Image courtesy of the Library of Congress, p. 33; © Herbert Gehr/Time Life Pictures/Getty Images, p. 34; GONE WITH THE WIND © Turner Entertainment Co. A Warner Bros. Entertainment Company. All Rights Reserved, p. 35; © MGM Studios, Image provided by Getty Images, p. 36; BRINGING UP BABY © RKO Pictures, Inc. Licensed by Warner Bros. Entertainment, Inc. All Rights Reserved, p. 37; © KING FEATURES SYNDICATE, Image provided by The Kobal Collection, p. 39; © John Kobal Foundation/Getty Images, p. 43; © Hulton-Deutsch Collection/CORBIS, p. 44; © H. Armstrong Roberts/Retrofile/Getty Images, pp. 45, 78; Courtesy of Universal Studios Licensing, LLLP, Image provided by The Kobal Collection, p. 49; THE GOOD EARTH © Turner Entertainment Co. A Warner Bros. Entertainment Company. All Rights Reserved, Image provided by Photofest, p. 53; Ad*Access On-Line Project. John W. Hartman Center for Sales, Advertising & Marketing History. Duke University Rare Book, Manuscript and Special Collections Library, pp. 56 (Ad # BH1738), 132 (Ad # BH1930); SEARS® Holdings Archives, p. 61; © McNEIL-PPC, Inc. 2007, Advertisement © 1930s. Used by permission, Image courtesy of The Advertising Archives, p. 62; SEARS® Holdings Archives, Image courtesy of the White River Valley Museum, p. 65; The Schlesinger Library, Radcliffe Institute, Harvard University, p. 77; Private Collection, p. 81 (both); © Tribune Media Services, Inc. All Rights Reserved. Reprinted with permission, Image courtesy of the Library of Congress, p. 82; The Estate of Margaret Bourke-White, p. 87; U.S. Food and Drug Administration, pp. 91, 92; The Illustrated London News, p. 94; *Miss Liberty*, Norman Rockwell, Photo courtesy of the Archives of the American Illustrators Gallery, NYC © Copyright 2007 National Museum of American Illustration, Newport, RI, www.americanillustration.org. Printed by permission of the Norman Rockwell Family Agency, Copyright © 1943 the Norman Rockwell Family Entities, p. 100; © CORBIS, pp. 102, 124; Courtesy Northwestern University Library, p. 106; © 1943 SEPS: Licensed by Curtis Publishing, Indianapolis, IN. All rights reserved. www.curtispublishing.com. Printed by permission of the Norman Rockwell Family Agency, Copyright © 1943 the Norman Rockwell Family Entities, p. 110; Image courtesy of the Special Collections Department, General Library, University of California, Davis, p. 113; © Photofest, p. 117 (top); Courtesy of the National Baseball Library and Archive, Cooperstown, NY, p. 118; National Archives Pacific Region, p. 123.

Front Cover: National Archives (left), © H. Armstrong Roberts/Retrofile/Getty Images (right).

About the Author

Catherine Gourley is an award-winning author and editor of books for young adults. A former editor of *Read* magazine, Gourley is the national director for Letters About Literature, a reading-writing promotion program of the Center for the Book in the Library of Congress. In addition, she is the curriculum writer for The Story of Movies, an educational outreach program on film study and visual literacy in the middle school developed by The Film Foundation, Los Angeles.

Among Gourley's more than 20 books are *Media Wizards* and *Society's Sisters* as well as the other four volumes in the Images and Issues of Women in the Twentieth Century series—*Gibson Girls and Suffragists: Perceptions of Women from 1900 to 1918*; *Flappers and the New American Woman: Perceptions of Women from 1918 through the 1920s*; *Gidgets and Women Warriors: Perceptions of Women in the 1950s and 1960s*; and *Ms. and the Material Girls: Perceptions of Women from the 1970s through the 1990s*.

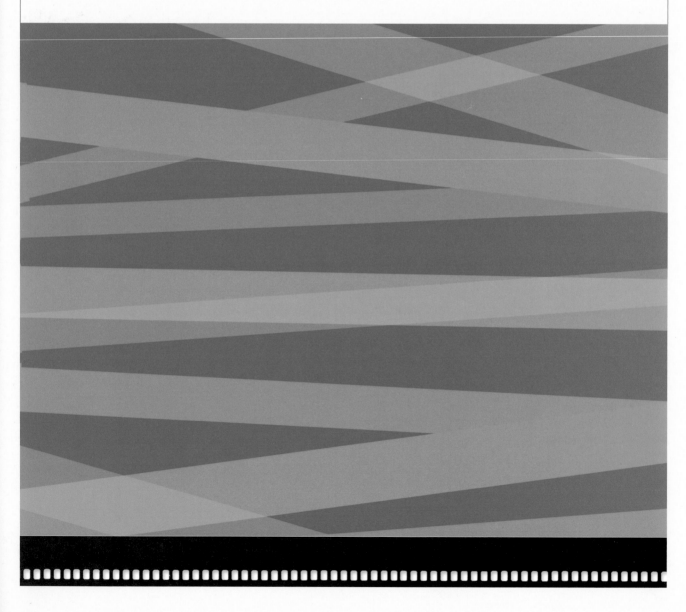